The Mathematics of
HOUSING
AND TAXES

Table of Contents

The Mathematics of Housing and Taxes, SV 9780547625645

Part III: Housing

Support Materials

The Mathematics of Housing and Taxes, SV 9780547625645

Introduction

The **Consumer Math** series is designed to help consumers understand mathematics as it relates to their everyday lives. Activities in this series help students not only understand the underlying mathematical concepts and equations they encounter day to day, but also helps them to be more financially savvy.

Each workbook in the series is divided into three sections and begins with a basic review of math concepts before moving on to more specific topics. Each section includes the following: Pre-Skills Test, Problem Solving Strategies, a Review, and a Test.

In addition, each workbook includes the following support material: Group projects, Practice forms, Charts, a Glossary, and an Answer Key.

The Mathematics of Housing and Taxes

The Mathematics of Housing and Taxes covers many of the principles of math that are faced when dealing with two of the most complicated expenses faced in everyday life. Part I serves as a basic review of fundamental math concepts. Part II focuses on calculating and reporting income and taxes. Part III concentrates on financial obligations involved with renting and owning property.

Part I: Math Skills and Concepts
- Whole Numbers
- Fractions, Decimals, & Percents
- Mean, Median, & Mode
- Basic Operations on a Calculator
- Computing Mentally
- Estimating

Part II: Taxes
- Reporting Income
- Federal Income Taxes
- Using Tax Form 1040EZ
- Itemized Deductions
- State and City Income Taxes
- Money Tips

Part III: Housing
- Renting an Apartment
- Buying a House
- Buying a Condominium
- Getting a Mortgage
- Real Estate Taxes
- Homeowner's Insurance
- Utilities
- Decorating & Remodeling
- Money Tips

Comprehensive Lessons

A **Pre-Skills Test** preceding each section helps teachers evaluate students' abilities and determine learning needs before beginning the lessons.

A wide variety of relevant exercises and activities engage students and keep them interested. Examples are motivated through real-world applications. Exercises include individual skills practice, mixed practice, and application problems.

Extension features offer more challenging problems related to the lesson's theme. **Calculator** activities present problems in which using a calculator is advantageous over paper and pencil. Interesting, real-life problems in **Think About It** spur class participation and provide additional opportunities to assess students' understanding.

Focused review and assessment opportunities are also included for each section.

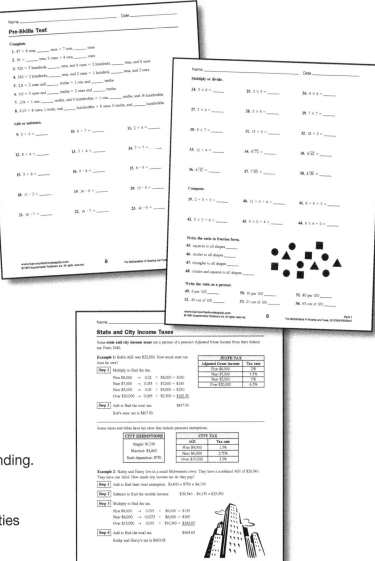

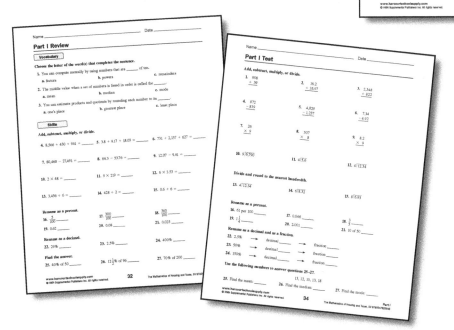

Extension Features

Money Tips examines the practical issues that affect buying decisions. Students look at factors that influence the cost of consumer goods as well as those that create consumer demand.

Mental Math helps students develop techniques to solve problems without using paper and pencil while reinforcing their confidence and estimation skills.

Estimation Skills extends students' understanding of estimation techniques and underscores their utility and practicality.

Calculator activities teach the keys and functions commonly available on calculators and emphasize the time-saving benefits.

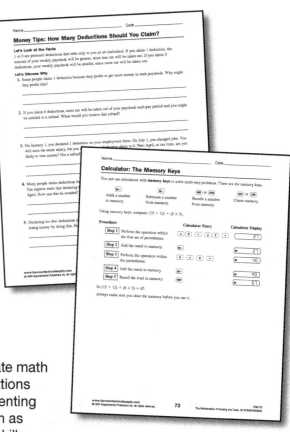

A Strong Base in Problem Solving

Multiple **Problem Solving Applications** in each book relate math skills to people, careers, and the world around us. Applications throughout the series address consumer topics, such as renting apartments and finding miles per gallon, and careers, such as pharmacist and carpenter, which require the use of math skills.

Each **Problem Solving Strategy** presents a realistic problem, a strategy, and a step-by-step approach to solving the problem. Practice exercises reinforce the strategy. Strategies include Drawing a Diagram, Using Estimation, Using a Map, and Working Backward.

Decision Making features offer open-ended lessons that reinforce logical reasoning and move beyond computation to a consideration of factors involved in making sound decisions. Lessons in the *Consumer Math* series include Choosing Transportation, Developing a Budget, Buying Stocks, and Choosing the Correct Tax Form.

Support Materials

Group Projects

Practice Forms

Charts

Glossary

Answer Key

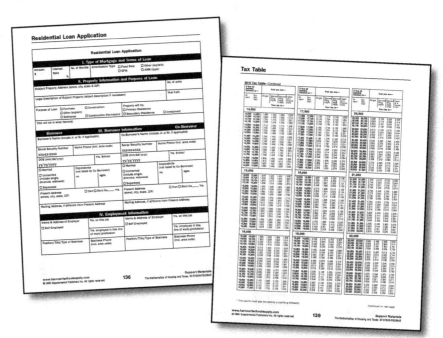

The Mathematics of Housing and Taxes, SV 9780547625645

Part I:
Math Skills and Concepts

Pre-Skills Test

Complete.

1. 87 = 8 tens, _____ ones = 7 tens, _____ ones

2. 59 = _____ tens, 9 ones = 4 tens, _____ ones

3. 326 = 3 hundreds, _____ tens, and 6 ones = 2 hundreds, _____ tens, and 6 ones

4. 242 = 2 hundreds, _____ tens, and 2 ones = 1 hundred, _____ tens, and 2 ones

5. 2.8 = 2 ones and _____ tenths = 1 one and _____ tenths

6. 3.6 = 3 ones and _____ tenths = 2 ones and _____ tenths

7. 1.74 = 1 one, _____ tenths, and 4 hundredths = 1 one, _____ tenths, and 14 hundredths

8. 8.13 = 8 ones, 1 tenth, and _____ hundredths = 8 ones, 0 tenths, and _____ hundredths

Add or subtract.

9. $5 + 3 =$ _____

10. $8 + 7 =$ _____

11. $2 + 4 =$ _____

12. $8 + 4 =$ _____

13. $3 + 4 =$ _____

14. $7 + 7 =$ _____

15. $3 + 6 =$ _____

16. $9 - 4 =$ _____

17. $6 - 3 =$ _____

18. $11 - 3 =$ _____

19. $14 - 6 =$ _____

20. $13 - 9 =$ _____

21. $16 - 7 =$ _____

22. $14 - 7 =$ _____

23. $14 - 9 =$ _____

8

Name _____ Date _____

Multiply or divide.

24. $5 \times 8 =$ _____

25. $3 \times 5 =$ _____

26. $4 \times 4 =$ _____

27. $3 \times 4 =$ _____

28. $5 \times 9 =$ _____

29. $7 \times 7 =$ _____

30. $8 \times 7 =$ _____

31. $15 \div 5 =$ _____

32. $18 \div 3 =$ _____

33. $32 \div 4 =$ _____

34. $9\overline{)72} =$ _____

35. $6\overline{)42} =$ _____

36. $4\overline{)32} =$ _____

37. $7\overline{)63} =$ _____

38. $8\overline{)56} =$ _____

Compute.

39. $2 + 5 + 3 =$ _____

40. $12 + 0 + 4 =$ _____

41. $8 + 9 + 3 =$ _____

42. $5 \times 3 + 6 =$ _____

43. $9 \times 0 + 4 =$ _____

44. $9 \times 4 + 0 =$ _____

Write the ratio in fraction form.

45. squares to all shapes _____

46. circles to all shapes _____

47. triangles to all shapes _____

48. circles and squares to all shapes _____

Write the ratio as a percent.

49. 6 per 100 _____

50. 16 per 100 _____

51. 80 per 100 _____

52. 49 out of 100 _____

53. 21 out of 100 _____

54. 93 out of 100 _____

The Mathematics of Housing and Taxes, SV 9780547625645

Adding and Subtracting Whole Numbers and Decimals

Addition and subtraction are related operations.

> Addend + Addend = Sum   Sum − Addend = Addend (= Difference)

Skill 1   Adding or subtracting whole numbers

(1a) Add 4,068 + 5,794

Step 1	**Step 2**	**Step 3**	**Step 4**
Add ones. Regroup.	Add tens. Regroup.	Add hundreds.	Add thousands.
$\begin{array}{r} \overset{1}{}4,068 \\ +\,5,794 \\ \hline 2 \end{array}$	$\begin{array}{r} \overset{1\,1}{}4,068 \\ +\,5,794 \\ \hline 62 \end{array}$	$\begin{array}{r} \overset{1\,1}{}4,068 \\ +\,5,794 \\ \hline 862 \end{array}$	$\begin{array}{r} \overset{1\,1}{}4,068 \\ +\,5,794 \\ \hline 9,862 \end{array}$

(1b) Subtract 8,674 − 6,319

Step 1	**Step 2**	**Step 3**	**Step 4**
Regroup tens. Subtract ones.	Subtract tens.	Subtract hundreds.	Subtract thousands.
$\begin{array}{r} \overset{6\,14}{8,6\cancel{7}\cancel{4}} \\ -\,6,319 \\ \hline 5 \end{array}$	$\begin{array}{r} \overset{6\,14}{8,6\cancel{7}\cancel{4}} \\ -\,6,319 \\ \hline 55 \end{array}$	$\begin{array}{r} \overset{6\,14}{8,6\cancel{7}\cancel{4}} \\ -\,6,319 \\ \hline 355 \end{array}$	$\begin{array}{r} \overset{6\,14}{8,6\cancel{7}\cancel{4}} \\ -\,6,319 \\ \hline 2,355 \end{array}$

Skill 2   Respect the position of the decimal point when adding or subtracting.

Subtract: 9.2 − 0.7

Step 1	**Step 2**	**Step 3**	**Step 4**
Line up the decimal points.	Write the decimal point for the difference.	Regroup ones. Subtract tenths.	Subtract ones.
$\begin{array}{r} 9.2 \\ -\,0.7 \\ \hline \end{array}$	$\begin{array}{r} 9.2 \\ -\,0.7 \\ \hline . \end{array}$	$\begin{array}{r} \overset{8\,12}{9\cancel{.}2} \\ -\,0.7 \\ \hline .5 \end{array}$	$\begin{array}{r} \overset{8\,12}{9\cancel{.}2} \\ -\,0.7 \\ \hline 8.5 \end{array}$

> **TIP** When lining up decimals, add zero as a placeholder, if necessary.
>
> Add 5.16 + 8.7 + 4.02
>
> $\begin{array}{r} 5.16 \\ 8.70 \\ +\,4.02 \\ \hline 17.88 \end{array}$

The Mathematics of Housing and Taxes, SV 9780547625645

Name _____   Date _____

Multiplying and Dividing Whole Numbers and Decimals

Factor × Factor = Product   Dividend ÷ Divisor = Quotient and (R) Remainder

Factor   Quotient (R) Remainder
×   Factor   Divisor⟌Dividend
Product

Skill 1   **Multiplying whole numbers**

Step 1

Multiply ones. Regroup.

$$\begin{array}{r} {}^{6}\\ 407 \\ \times\quad 9 \\ \hline 3 \end{array}$$

Step 2

Multiply tens. Then add 6 tens.
THINK: 0 tens + 6 tens = 6 tens

$$\begin{array}{r} {}^{6}\\ 407 \\ \times\quad 9 \\ \hline 63 \end{array}$$

Step 3

Multiply hundreds.

$$\begin{array}{r} {}^{6}\\ 407 \\ \times\quad 9 \\ \hline 3{,}663 \end{array}$$

Skill 2   **Multiplying whole numbers and decimals**

Step 1

Multiply as you would whole numbers.

$$\begin{array}{r} 1.73 \\ \times\quad 8 \\ \hline 1384 \end{array}$$

Step 2

Count the number of decimal places in the factors. There are that many decimal places in the product.

$$\begin{array}{rl} 1.73 & \text{2 decimal places} \\ \times\quad 8 & \text{0 decimal places} \\ \hline 13.84 & \text{2 decimal places} \end{array}$$

Skill 3   **Dividing decimals by whole numbers**

Step 1 Place the decimal point in the quotient directly above the decimal point in the dividend.

Step 2 Divide as you would whole numbers. Write additional zeros in the dividend as needed.

$$\begin{array}{r} 3.05 \\ 6\,⟌\overline{18.30} \\ \underline{18} \\ 3 \\ \underline{0} \\ 30 \\ \underline{30} \\ 0 \end{array}$$

TIP   **Rounding the quotient:**

Rounding to the hundredths   0.485 ≈ 0.49
Rounding to the tenths   0.485 ≈ 0.5
Remember: ≈ means approximately equal to.

The Mathematics of Housing and Taxes, SV 9780547625645

Name _____   Date _____

Practice

Add, subtract, multiply, or divide.

1.
   2.5
   + 29.63

2.
   802
   311
   + 89

3.
   13.2
   14.57
   + 0.7

4. 964
   − 87

5.
   69.5
   − 34.28

6.
   85.21
   − 32.3

7. 609
   × 5

8.
   4.32
   × 2

9.
   7.07
   × 4

10. 2)37

11. 7)6.3

12. 5)0.52

13. 4,892 + 3,605 = _____

14. 2,053 + 87 + 763 = _____

15. 9.6 + 13.05 + 10 = _____

16. 937 − 425 = _____

17. 58.32 − 29.54 = _____

18. 90.08 − 69.79 = _____

19. 3 × 221 = _____

20. 8 × 0.65 = _____

21. 4 × 0.09 = _____

22. 83 ÷ 4 = _____

23. 6,790 ÷ 9 = _____

24. 12.34 ÷ 4 = _____

Divide and round to the nearest tenth.

25. 9.92 ÷ 4 = _____

26. 5.48 ÷ 8 = _____

Divide and round to the nearest hundredth.

27. 8.59 ÷ 4 = _____

28. 6.87 ÷ 7 = _____

The Mathematics of Housing and Taxes, SV 9780547625645

Solve.

29. It is 789 miles from Houston, Texas to Atlanta, Georgia, and 2,496 miles from Atlanta to San Francisco, California. How many miles is it total from Houston to Atlanta and then on to San Francisco? _____

30. Ron spent $28.36 at the sports store and $16.09 at the deli. How much did he spend all together? _____

31. It is 2,078 miles from Dallas, Texas to Seattle, Washington. You have already traveled 1,693 miles. How many more miles do you need to travel? _____

32. You need to buy some school supplies. The total cost of the supplies is $9.06. You have $7.98. How much more money do you need? _____

33. It is 379 miles from Los Angeles to San Francisco. You made this trip 7 times. How many miles did you travel in all? _____

34. Your class is selling school shirts for $15.75 each. The class sold 8 shirts during the first hour of the sale. How much money was collected during that hour? _____

35. An 8-oz box of chocolates costs $9.60. How much is the cost per ounce? _____

36. It is about 2,628 miles from Los Angeles to Washington, D.C. You made the trip in 6 days, traveling the same distance each day. How many miles did you travel each day? _____

Fractions, Decimals, and Percents

Skill 1   Renaming decimals as percents

Rename 0.9 as a percent.

Step 1	Multiply by 100 by moving the decimal point 2 places to the right. Write additional zeros if necessary.	$0.90 \longrightarrow 90.0$
Step 2	Write the percent sign.	90%

Other examples

$0.89 \longrightarrow 0.89 \longrightarrow 89\%$ $0.034 \longrightarrow 0.034 \longrightarrow 3.4\%$ $8.4 \longrightarrow 8.40 \longrightarrow 840\%$

Skill 2   Renaming fractions as percents

Rename $\frac{1}{5}$ as a percent.

Step 1	Write the fraction as a decimal. Divide the numerator by the denominator. Write additional zeros if necessary.	$\frac{1}{5} \longrightarrow 5\overline{)\begin{array}{c} 0.2 \\ 1.0 \end{array}}$
Step 2	Write the decimal as a percent.	$0.20 \longrightarrow 20\%$

Skill 3   Renaming percents as decimals

Rename 3% as a decimal.

Step 1	Divide by 100 by moving the decimal point 2 places to the left. Write additional zeros if necessary.	$3\% \longrightarrow 0.03\%$
Step 2	Remove the percent sign.	0.03

Other examples

$43\% \longrightarrow 0.43\% \longrightarrow 0.43$ $5.7\% \longrightarrow 0.05.7\% \longrightarrow 0.057$ $287\% \longrightarrow 2.87\% \longrightarrow 2.87$

Skill 4   Renaming percents as fractions

Rename 80% as a fraction.

| **Step 1** | Write the percent as a fraction with a denominator of 100. | $80\% = \dfrac{80}{100}$ |

| **Step 2** | Write the fraction in lowest terms. | $\dfrac{80}{100} = \dfrac{80 \div 20}{100 \div 20} = \dfrac{4}{5}$ |

Other examples

$75\% = \dfrac{75}{100} = \dfrac{75 \div 25}{100 \div 25} = \dfrac{3}{4}$ $150\% = \dfrac{150}{100} = \dfrac{150 \div 50}{100 \div 50} = \dfrac{3}{2} = 1\dfrac{1}{2}$

Skill 5   Expressing percents as decimals

Any percent can be expressed as a decimal.

Find 40% of 19.

| **Step 1** | Write the problem as a number sentence. | 40% of 19 is _____ $\longrightarrow$ $40\% \times 19 =$ _____ |

| **Step 2** | Rename the percent as a decimal. **THINK:** $40\% = 0.40 = 0.4$ | $0.4 \times 19 =$ _____ |

| **Step 3** | Solve. | $0.4 \times 19 = 7.6$ |

Skill 6   Expressing percents as fractions

Sometimes it is easier to express a percent as a fraction.

Find 75% of 16.

| **Step 1** | Write the problem as a number sentence. | 75% of 16 is _____ $\longrightarrow$ $75\% \times 16 =$ _____ |

| **Step 2** | Rename the percent as a fraction. **THINK:** $75\% = \dfrac{3}{4}$ | $\dfrac{3}{4} \times 16 =$ _____ |

| **Step 3** | Solve. **THINK:** $\dfrac{1}{4} \times 16 \longrightarrow 16 \div 4 = 4$ $\dfrac{3}{4} \times 16 \longrightarrow 3 \times 4 = 12$ $\dfrac{3}{4} \times 16 = 12$ So 75% of 16 is 12. | |

Practice

Rename as a percent.

1. $\dfrac{23}{100}$ = _____

2. $\dfrac{7}{100}$ = _____

3. $\dfrac{186}{100}$ = _____

4. 0.63 = _____

5. 0.058 = _____

6. 9 = _____

Rename as a decimal and as a percent.

7. $\dfrac{1}{4}$ = _____ = _____

8. $\dfrac{7}{8}$ = _____ = _____

9. $\dfrac{2}{5}$ = _____ = _____

10. $3\dfrac{1}{2}$ = _____ = _____

11. $9\dfrac{1}{8}$ = _____ = _____

12. $5\dfrac{3}{5}$ = _____ = _____

Rename as a decimal.

13. 24% = _____

14. 18% = _____

15. 2% = _____

16. 2.8% = _____

17. 0.05% = _____

18. 438% = _____

Rename as a fraction. Write fractions in lowest terms.

19. 70% = _____

20. 40% = _____

21. 85% = _____

22. 110% = _____

23. 187% = _____

24. 204% = _____

Find the answer. Decide whether to express the percent as a decimal or as a fraction.

25. 10% of 40 = _____

26. 25% of 24 = _____

27. 80% of 50 = _____

28. 40% of 15 = _____

29. 75% of 56 = _____

30. $33\dfrac{1}{3}$% of 36 = _____

31. $87\dfrac{1}{2}$% of 72 = _____

32. 50% of 73 = _____

33. $16\dfrac{2}{3}$% of 36 = _____

34. $37\dfrac{1}{2}$% of 64 = _____

35. 2% of 95 = _____

36. $33\dfrac{1}{3}$% of 39 = _____

Name _____ Date _____

Solve.

37. The trip between 2 towns is exactly 90 miles. You have gone 40% of this distance. How far have you gone? _____

38. Rosa received a grade of 88% on her vocabulary test. There were 25 fill-in-the-blank questions on the test. How many questions did Rosa get correct? _____

39. It takes Cara 35 minutes to walk to school. It takes Sue 80% of Cara's time. How long does it take Sue? _____

40. A sports watch originally cost $144. It is now being sold for 85% of its original price. How much does the watch cost now? _____

41. A wetsuit originally cost $750. It is now being sold at 30% off. How much has been deducted from the original cost of the wetsuit? _____

42. After a taste test, 40% of the 30 people interviewed preferred a new energy drink over orange juice. The rest preferred orange juice.

a. How many people preferred the energy drink? _____

b. How many people preferred orange juice? _____

Problem Solving Strategy: Interpreting Data from Tables and Graphs

Situation:

The sales staff at Donney Motors keeps records of their car and truck sales. Contests are sometimes held to encourage special efforts to sell various cars and trucks. How can these records be used to identify a salesperson's performance?

Strategy:

You can use information in a **table** or a **bar graph** to solve a problem.

Applying the Strategy:

A. The salesperson who sold the greatest number of trucks in October won a flat-screen T.V. Who was it?

THINK: Look at the column labeled "Number of Trucks Sold."

October Sales	
Salesperson	**Number of Trucks Sold**
Ruth	22
Art	15
John	9
Eric	12
Mindy	4

Step 1 Which number is the greatest? (22)

Step 2 Which name is on the same line as 22? (Ruth)

Ruth sold the greatest number of trucks in October and won the TV.

B. Eric sold the greatest number of cars and trucks last year and won a free trip. How many cars and trucks did he sell?

THINK: Look at the bar above Eric's name.

Step 1 Between which 2 numbers does the bar lie? (250 and 300)

Step 2 Is the bar nearer to 250 or 300? (It is halfway between 250 and 300.)

Step 3 What number is halfway between 250 and 300? (250 + 300 = 550) (550 ÷ 2 = 275)

Eric sold 275 cars and trucks last year.

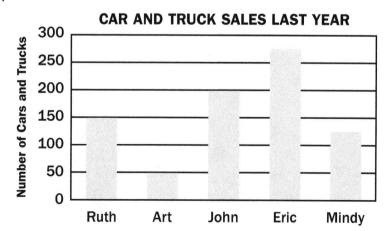

CAR AND TRUCK SALES LAST YEAR

Name _____ Date _____

Practice

Use the table of December sales for problems 1–2.

1. How many cars did Art sell? _____

2. How many more cars did John sell than Ruth?

   _____

December Sales	
Salesperson	**Number of Cars Sold**
Ruth	15
Art	25
John	30
Ginger	25
Eric	10
Mindy	20

The sales staff posted a bar graph to show the numbers of cars and trucks Donney Motors leased last year. Use the bar graph to answer problems 3–4.

3. How many 4-door sedans were leased? _____

4. How many more pick-up trucks were leased than 2-door sedans?

   _____

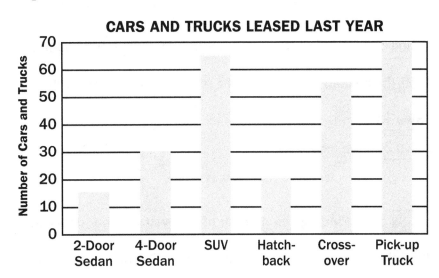

5. Use the information in the "December Sales" table at the top of the page to construct a bar graph. Use this vertical scale: 0, 5, 10, 15, 20, 25, 30, 35.

_____

Mean, Median, and Mode

> **Mean (average)**—The sum of a group of numbers divided by the number of addends.
> **Median**—The middle number when a group of numbers is arranged in order from least to greatest.
> **Mode**—The number that occurs most frequently in a group of numbers.

Skill 1   Finding the mean

Find the mean of these basketball players' scores: 48, 36, 51, 72, 58.

| Step 1 | Add the scores. | $48 + 36 + 51 + 72 + 58 = 265$ |
| Step 2 | Divide by the number of scores. | $265 \div 5 = 53$ |

The mean, or average, of these scores is 53.

Skill 2   Finding the median of an odd number of scores

Find the median of these bowling scores: 126, 108, 145, 108, 117.

| Step 1 | Arrange the scores in order. | 108   108   117   126   145 |
| Step 2 | Find the middle score. | 117 |

The median of these scores is 117.

Skill 3   Finding the median of an even number of scores

Find the median of these bowling scores: 139, 106, 145, 113, 128, 109.

Step 1	Arrange the scores in order.	106 109 113 128 139 145
Step 2	Find the middle score. (**THINK:** There is no *one* middle number.)	113 128
Step 3	Find the mean of the two middle scores.	$113 + 128 = 241 \div 2 = 120.5$

The median of these scores is 120.5.

Skill 4   Finding the mode

Find the mode of these race times: 9.3, 9.6, 9.2, 10.2, 9.6, 10.1, 9.5.

Find the time that occurs most often.   9.6 occurs twice

The mode of these scores is 9.6.

Name _____ Date _____

Practice

Find the mean.

1. 86, 90, 94 _____

2. 4.2, 8.5, 2.6 _____

3. 172, 550, 293, 413 _____

4. 95, 63, 12, 102 _____

5. 20, 18, 6, 10, 16 _____

6. 0.18, 0.45, 0.34, 0.51, 0.27 _____

Find the median.

7. 7, 13, 25, 46, 8 _____

8. 9, 12, 7, 24, 18 _____

9. 1.3, 6.2, 8.9, 2.4, 5.6 _____

10. 1.3, 5.2, 4.7, 1.6, 4.1, 7.3 _____

Find the mode.

11. 1, 3, 5, 9, 3, 6, 7, 8 _____

12. 9.6, 4.5, 1.8, 4.7, 6.7, 1.8, 3.2 _____

Find the mean, the median, and the mode. Round the mean and median to the nearest tenth.

13. 56, 78, 92   mean _____   median _____   mode _____

14. 6.3, 2.5, 10.1   mean _____   median _____   mode _____

15. 302, 220, 220, 208   mean _____   median _____   mode _____

16. 75, 93, 89, 75, 84   mean _____   median _____   mode _____

17. 6.1, 5.9, 4.2, 5.9, 10.7   mean _____   median _____   mode _____

Solve.

18. Six judges scored a diving contest. On one dive, 2 judges gave a 7.5. The other scores were 8.0, 7.9, 6.8, and 7.3. What are the mean, median, and mode of these scores?

mean _____   median _____   mode _____

| Extension | Using a Tally |

Each time Ed played miniature golf, he made a tally mark next to his score.

1. How many games did Ed play? _____

2. What are his two mode scores? _____

3. What is his median score? _____

4. What is the total of the scores of:
   (a) 69? _____; (b) 68? _____; (c) 67? _____

5. What is his mean score? _____

Score	Total	Score	Total
72 - II	144	69 - ⲦⲎⳒ II	
71 - II	142	68 - ⲦⲎⳒ II	
70 - III	210	67 - II	

Basic Operations on a Calculator

When you want to compute quickly and accurately with greater numbers, you can use a calculator.

The four basic operations (addition, subtraction, multiplication, and division) can be performed easily.

Operation	Calculator Entry	Calculator Display
Add: 49,567 + 78,078	[4] [9] [5] [6] [7] [+] [7] [8] [0] [7] [8] [=]	127.645
Subtract: 34.014 − 5.708	[3] [4] [.] [0] [1] [4] [−] [5] [.] [7] [0] [8] [=]	28.306
Multiply: 908 × 0.045	[9] [0] [8] [×] [0] [.] [0] [4] [5] [=]	40.86
Divide: 4.9452 ÷ 0.078	[4] [.] [9] [4] [5] [2] [÷] [0] [.] [0] [7] [8] [=]	63.4

You can use a calculator to do a series of operations without using the [=] **key (is equal to)** after each operation.

Operation	Calculator Entry	Calculator Display
1. Subtract.	[4] [5] [.] [0] [9] [−] [6] [+] ↑ Get ready to subtract.	39.09
2. Add.	[4] [.] [7] [−] ↑ Get ready to subtract.	43.79
3. Subtract.	[1] [8] [=]	25.79

So, 45.09 − 6 + 4.7 − 18 = 25.79.

TIP The [CE] **key (Clear Entry)** can help you when you have entered a wrong number into the calculator.

Name _____ Date _____

1. For which operations will the order in which you enter two numbers not affect the answer? Why?

_____

2. The entry below was made on two different calculators. One calculator displayed the answer 6.15. The other calculator displayed the answer 16.4. Explain the different answers.

$$\boxed{4}\ \boxed{.}\ \boxed{5}\ \boxed{\times}\ \boxed{3}\ \boxed{+}\ \boxed{7}\ \boxed{-}\ \boxed{8}\ \boxed{.}\ \boxed{2}\ \boxed{\div}\ \boxed{2}\ \boxed{=}$$

_____

_____

Practice

Use a calculator to compute.

1. $1{,}394{,}588 - 246{,}183 = $ _____

2. $4{,}496 + 2{,}739 = $ _____

3. $27{,}600 \div 48 = $ _____

4. $722.5 - 23.667 = $ _____

5. $416.30 \times 17.6 = $ _____

6. $44.73 \times 6.05 \div 2 = $ _____

7. 45.2 divided into 85,880 = _____

8. 0.3 divided into 0.021 = _____

Divide and round to the nearest tenth.

9. $18.6\overline{)340}$

10. $3.99\overline{)465}$

Divide and round to the nearest hundredth.

11. $0.45 \div 3.6 = $ _____

12. $51.2\overline{)3.115}$

Compute from left to right.

13. $824.8 - 4.723 + 364.9 - 283.69 = $ _____

14. $45.36 \div 0.3 \times 0.45 \div 15 = $ _____

Solve.

15. Joe's car odometer read 27,314 miles when he left for vacation. Three weeks later, the odometer read 32,563 miles. How far had Joe traveled? _____

16. Gary ordered 500 sheets of paper. When they arrived, they formed a pile 4.2 centimeters high. How thick was each sheet? _____

Computing Mentally

You may often find it easier to compute mentally than to use a pencil and paper or even a calculator. You can add mentally by using numbers that are **multiples of 10** and then adjusting.

Example 1: You are buying a shirt for $19 and a jacket for $44. Mentally compute the cost of the shirt and the jacket.

Add: $19 + $44

THINK: $19 is $1 less than $20. $20 + $44 = $64

So $19 + $44 is $1 less than $64, or $63.

The shirt and the jacket will cost $63.

You can subtract mentally in the same way.

Example 2: Subtract:

  a. 94 − 18

    THINK: 18 is 2 less than 20.

    94 − 20 = 74
    So 94 − 18 is 2 more than 74, or 76.

  b. 465 − 190

    THINK: 190 is 10 less than 200.

    465 − 200 = 265
    So 465 − 190 is 10 more than 265, or 275.

Mental computation is also commonly used when you multiply or divide by **powers of 10**, such as 10, 100, or 1,000.

Example 3: Multiply: 100 × 87.30

THINK: The product must be greater than 87.3, so move the decimal point to the right.

    100 × 87.30 = 8,730

  2 zeros
        2 places right

Example 4: Divide: 38,430 ÷ 1,000

THINK: The quotient must be less than 38,430, so move the decimal point to the left.

    38,430 ÷ 1,000 = 38.43

  3 places left
        3 zeros

Name _____   Date _____

1. Ricky argues that mental computation is a waste of time, since he has a calculator. How would you convince Ricky that he is wrong?

_____

_____

Practice

Use mental computation to add or subtract.

1. $49 + 14 =$ _____

2. $35 + 28 =$ _____

3. $397 + 220 =$ _____

4. $46¢ + 19¢ =$ _____

5. $\$4.52 + \$5.19 =$ _____

6. $5.27 + 3.09 =$ _____

7. $67 - 13 =$ _____

8. $374 - 229 =$ _____

9. $40¢ - 34¢ =$ _____

10. $\$975 - \$580 =$ _____

11. $\$1.20 - \$0.81 =$ _____

12. $3.77 - 2.12 =$ _____

Use mental computation to multiply or divide.

13. $100 \times 5.3 =$ _____

14. $10 \times 0.532 =$ _____

15. $100 \times 578.5 =$ _____

16. $18.3 \div 10 =$ _____

17. $25.5 \div 100 =$ _____

18. $2,066 \div 100 =$ _____

Solve using mental computation.

19. A $750 washing machine is marked down by $159. How much does the dishwasher now sell for?
_____

20. The 100 members of a marching band agree to split the $7,850.00 cost of their trip. What is each member's share? _____

Multiplying Mentally by 50 and by 25

Multiply: 50×2.8
THINK: $100 \times 2.8 = 280$
Since $50 = 100 \div 2$, then $50 \times 2.8 = 280 \div 2 = 140$.

Multiply: 25×16.4
THINK: $100 \times 16.4 = 1,640$
Since $25 = 100 \div 4$, then $25 \times 16.4 = 1,640 \div 4 = 410$.

Use mental computation to multiply.

1. $50 \times 62 =$ _____

2. $25 \times 220 =$ _____

3. $50 \times 110 =$ _____

Estimating Sums and Differences

A common way to **estimate** sums is to round each number to the same **place value** and then add mentally.

Example 1: About how much is the total population of Fairview County?

Town	Greenfield	Salem	Goshen	Wells
Population	21,284	3,487	38,372	10,480

Step 1 Round each number to the thousands place.

$$
\begin{array}{rcr}
21,284 & \longrightarrow & 21,000 \\
3,487 & \longrightarrow & 3,000 \\
38,372 & \longrightarrow & 38,000 \\
+\ 10,480 & \longrightarrow & +\ 10,000 \\
\hline
 & & 72,000
\end{array}
$$

Step 2 Add.

72,000 is a good estimate for the total population.

Example 2:

a. Estimate: 31.07 + 0.6 + 3.87

Step 1 Round each number to the tenths place.

$$
\begin{array}{rcr}
31.07 & \longrightarrow & 31.1 \\
0.6 & \longrightarrow & 0.6 \\
+\ 3.87 & \longrightarrow & +\ 3.9 \\
\hline
 & & 35.6
\end{array}
$$

Step 2 Add.

b. Estimate: 95¢ + $2.09 + $5.75

Step 1 Round each number to the ones place.

$$
\begin{array}{rcr}
\$0.95 & \longrightarrow & \$1 \\
\$2.09 & \longrightarrow & \$2 \\
+\ \$5.75 & \longrightarrow & +\ \$6 \\
\hline
 & & \$9
\end{array}
$$

Step 2 Add.

The same estimating rules are used for subtraction.

Example 3:

a. Estimate: 27,387 − 2,163

Step 1 Round each number to the nearest thousands place.

$$
\begin{array}{rcr}
27,387 & \longrightarrow & 27,000 \\
-\ 2,163 & \longrightarrow & -\ 2,000 \\
\hline
 & & 25,000
\end{array}
$$

Step 2 Subtract.

b. Estimate: 0.37 − 0.097

Step 1 Round each number to the tenths place.

$$
\begin{array}{rcr}
0.37 & \longrightarrow & 0.4 \\
-\ 0.097 & \longrightarrow & -\ 0.1 \\
\hline
 & & 0.3
\end{array}
$$

Step 2 Subtract.

Name _____ Date _____

Think About It

1. How is mental computation different from estimation?

_____

_____

2. To estimate $4.80 + $2.25 + $3.40, Gail used $5 + $2 + $3 = $10. Gail's mother rounded up and used $5 + $3 + 4 = $12. What are some advantages of doing estimation the second way?

_____

_____

Practice

Estimate the sum or difference to the place value indicated.

1. 356   (hundreds)
    + 149

2. 562   (tens)
    618
    + 74

3. $6.44   (ones)
    + $3.04

4. $2.58   (ones)
    $0.75
    + $1.77

5. 794.5   (tens)
    + 57.19

6. 0.073   (tenths)
    + 0.99

7. 27,899   (thousands)
    + 9,821

8. 0.031   (thousandths)
    + 0.0021

9. 292   (tens)
    − 17

10. 68,391   (ten thousands)
    − 23,512

11. $1.42   (tenths)
    − $0.57

12. $17.32   (tenths)
    − $0.34

13. 201.42   (tens)
    − 34.09

14. 4.39   (tenths)
    − 0.15

15. $719.17   (ones)
    − $3.06

Solve.

16. Julie bought a sandwich for $7.17. About how much change did she get from $10.00? _____

17. A pair of shoes is advertised at a shoe store for $379. The same shoe is on sale at Discount Den for $285. About how much can be saved by buying the shoes at Discount Den? _____

Estimating Products and Quotients

A common way to estimate products and quotients is to round each number to its **greatest place** and then compute mentally.

Example 1: There were 285 wildlife pamphlets left to be distributed. Six friends shared the task. About how many pamphlets must each person hand out if they share the job?

| **Step 1** | Round. | 285 rounds to 300. Since 6 is a 1-digit number, it does not need to be rounded. |

| **Step 2** | Divide. | $300 \div 6 = 50$. |

So each person will hand out about 50 pamphlets.

Example 2:

  a. Estimate: $2,789 \times 48$

| **Step 1** | Round. | $3,000 \times 50$ |
| **Step 2** | Multiply. | 150,000 |

  b. Estimate: $22,270 \div 39$

| **Step 1** | Round. | $20,000 \div 40$ |
| **Step 2** | Divide. | 500 |

When multiplying or dividing decimals or money amounts, estimate by rounding each number to its **greatest nonzero place**.

Example 3:

  a. Estimate: $78 \times \$0.29$

| **Step 1** | Round. | $80 \times \$0.30$ |
| **Step 2** | Multiply. | \$24 |

  b. Estimate: $324.8 \div 4.87$

| **Step 1** | Round. | $300 \div 5$ |
| **Step 2** | Divide. | 60 |

Think About It

1. Laura calculated that 3.2×16.8 is 5.376. Estimate and explain why Laura's answer cannot be correct.

_____

_____

_____

Practice

Estimate the product and quotient.

1. $4,822 \times 45 \approx$ _____

2. $51 \times \$12.65 \approx$ _____

3. $350 \times \$18.95 \approx$ _____

4. $72 \times 5.3 \approx$ _____

5. $8.8 \times 3.23 \approx$ _____

6. $26.19 \times 7.47 \approx$ _____

7. $375 \times \$0.72 \approx$ _____

8. $195 \times 0.89 \approx$ _____

9. $0.55 \times 0.34 \approx$ _____

10. $206 \div 39 \approx$ _____

11. $865 \div 172 \approx$ _____

12. $\$14.80 \div 5 \approx$ _____

13. $\$42.30 \div 22 \approx$ _____

14. $\$283 \div 43 \approx$ _____

15. $97 \div 1.87 \approx$ _____

16. $927.5 \div 46 \approx$ _____

17. $25.7 \div 5.4 \approx$ _____

18. $982.1 \div 19.3 \approx$ _____

Use the menu for problems 19–20.

19. About how much will 3 juices cost? _____

20. About how many hamburgers can be bought for $12.00? _____

MENU	
Hamburgers	$2.89
Hot Dogs	$2.15
Chicken Sandwich	$3.49
Salad	$2.50
Juice	$1.19
Apple Slices	$0.79
Popcorn	$0.75

Solve.

21. Designer plates cost $9.75 each. About how much will 12 plates cost? _____

22. Winter coats cost $199.00 each. About how many coats can be bought for $900.00? _____

Name _____ Date _____

Problem Solving Strategy: Which Way to Compute?

Situation:
Suppose you are asked to find the cost of 5 pairs of socks at $1.95 a pair plus a sales tax of $0.40. Which way would you use to compute the answer?

Strategy:
Use paper and pencil skills, a calculator, or mental computation skills depending on the situation, the numbers involved, or your own personal preference.

Applying the Strategy:

Joan took out a pencil and computed:

$$\begin{array}{r} \$1.95 \\ \times\ \ \ \ 5 \\ \hline \$9.75 \\ +\ \ 0.40 \\ \hline \$10.15 \end{array}$$

Jill took out a calculator and computed:

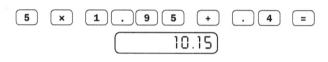

Jackie thought:

$1.95 is 5¢ less than $2. So 5 pairs are 25¢ less than $10, or $9.75, plus 40¢.

40¢ is 25¢ plus 15¢. So $9.75 plus 25¢ is $10, plus 15¢ is $10.15.

Notice that Joan, Jill, and Jackie all got the same answer.

Other Situations:

A. What is the best way to compute the amount of change that Ray received if he paid $5.00 for a $2.97 meal?

Ray can easily compute this mentally.
He thinks: $2.97 is 3¢ less than $3.00.
$5.00 − $3.00 is $2.00.

So $5.00 − $2.97 is $2.00 plus 3¢, or $2.03.

B. What is the best way for Alvin to compute the new balance in the class treasury? The balance was $357.82. He made a deposit of $182.14 and then made a withdrawal of $78.50.

Alvin needs an exact answer, and the numbers are too great to use mental computation. So he uses his calculator or paper and pencil to get $461.46.

C. What is the best way for Mr. Lee to compute the total length of pipe? One piece is $4\frac{3}{4}$ feet long, and the other is $2\frac{7}{8}$ feet long.

If Mr. Lee wants an exact answer, it is unlikely that he will use mental computation or convert to decimals and use a calculator. He will probably use paper and pencil.

$$\begin{array}{rcl} 4\frac{3}{4} & = & 4\frac{6}{8} \\ +\ 2\frac{7}{8} & = & +\ 2\frac{7}{8} \\ \hline & & 6\frac{13}{8} = 7\frac{5}{8} \text{ feet} \end{array}$$

Think About It

1. Show how Alvin could have solved his problem with paper and pencil instead of a calculator. Discuss which method you prefer and why.

_____

_____

_____

_____

2. Show how Mr. Lee could have solved his problem using a calculator. Discuss why this answer is different from what Mr. Lee found.

_____

_____

_____

_____

Practice

Identify whether you would most likely use paper and pencil, a calculator, or mental computation to compute.

1. Find the number of 2-foot planks in a 12-foot board. _____

2. Find the trip mileage, using a map. _____

3. Find the monthly mortgage payment on a loan amount of $150,000. _____

4. Find the average weight of 10 pieces of fruit. _____

Use two different methods to compute. Identify the most efficient method.

5. The actual distance between two cities that are $3\frac{1}{4}$ inches apart on a map with a scale of 1 inch per 40 miles.

6. The cost per person if 7 people spent a total of $199.99 on dinner.

Part I Review

Vocabulary

Choose the letter of the word(s) that completes the sentence.

1. You can compute mentally by using numbers that are _____ of ten.

   a. factors   **b.** powers   **c.** remainders

2. The middle value when a set of numbers is listed in order is called the _____.

   a. mean   **b.** median   **c.** mode

3. You can estimate products and quotients by rounding each number to its _____.

   a. one's place   **b.** greatest place   **c.** least place

Skills

Add, subtract, multiply, or divide.

4. $8{,}566 + 430 + 941 =$ _____   5. $3.8 + 9.17 + 18.03 =$ _____   6. $731 + 2{,}137 + 627 =$ _____

7. $80{,}468 - 27{,}491 =$ _____   8. $64.3 - 53.76 =$ _____   9. $12.07 - 9.41 =$ _____

10. $2 \times 48 =$ _____   11. $9 \times 219 =$ _____   12. $6 \times 3.53 =$ _____

13. $3{,}456 \div 6 =$ _____   14. $428 \div 2 =$ _____   15. $0.6 \div 6 =$ _____

Rename as a percent.

16. $\frac{5}{100}$ _____   17. $\frac{300}{100}$ _____   18. $\frac{365}{100}$ _____

19. 0.62 _____   20. 0.08 _____   21. 0.025 _____

Rename as a decimal.

22. 29% _____   23. 2.5% _____   24. 400% _____

Find the answer.

25. 40% of 50 _____   26. $12\frac{1}{2}\%$ of 96 _____   27. 70% of 200 _____

Use a calculator to compute.

28. $4{,}289 + 7{,}873 + 172 =$ _____

29. $57.93 \times 33.58 =$ _____

30. $7 + 34.88 - 12.938 =$ _____

31. $10.5 \times 31.22 \div 16.4 =$ _____

Compute mentally.

32. $357 + 292 =$ _____

33. $10 \times 9.3 =$ _____

34. $522 \div 100 =$ _____

35. $65{,}778 \div 1{,}000 =$ _____

Estimate.

36. $6{,}735 + 3{,}221 \approx$ _____

37. $14.89 - 3.902 \approx$ _____

38. $0.44 \times 0.07 \approx$ _____

39. $68 \div 2 \approx$ _____

40. $2\frac{2}{3} + 32\frac{1}{4} \approx$ _____

41. $8\frac{4}{5} - 2\frac{1}{3} \approx$ _____

Solve.

42. A traveling athlete drove 553 miles to events in April. In May, she drove 1,108 miles to events, and in June, 598 miles to events. What was the total number of miles that the athlete drove to events during these 3 months? _____

43. A textile manufacturer must finish filling an order for 2,020 yards of fabric. He has already shipped 950 yards. How many more yards must he ship? _____

44. Garza cut a $17\frac{3}{8}$-inch board from a board $40\frac{1}{2}$ inches long. About how much wood is left?

_____

45. Fancy peaches are on sale for $16.79 a bushel (tax included). Will $50 be enough to buy 3 bushels?

_____

Name _____   Date _____

Part I Test

Add, subtract, multiply, or divide.

1. 908
    + 39

2. 16.2
    + 35.97

3. 2,348
    + 822

4. 872
    − 839

5. 4,829
    − 1,237

6. 7.34
    − 4.92

7. 26
    × 9

8. 307
    × 8

9. 8.2
    × 9

10. $9\overline{)6{,}790}$

11. $4\overline{)5.6}$

12. $4\overline{)12.34}$

Divide and round to the nearest hundredth.

13. $4\overline{)12.34}$

14. $6\overline{)8.32}$

15. $8\overline{)6.93}$

Rename as a percent.

16. 61 per 100 _____

17. 0.046 _____

18. $\frac{3}{5}$ _____

19. $1\frac{1}{4}$ _____

20. 2.001 _____

21. 10 of 50 _____

Rename as a decimal and as a fraction.

22. 2.5%   ⟶   decimal _____   ⟶   fraction _____

23. 50%   ⟶   decimal _____   ⟶   fraction _____

24. 150%   ⟶   decimal _____   ⟶   fraction _____

Use the following numbers to answer questions 25–27.

13, 12, 10, 13, 18

25. Find the mean: _____

26. Find the median: _____

27. Find the mode: _____

Name _____ Date _____

Use a calculator to compute.

28. $8{,}622 + 1{,}387 =$ _____   **29.** $15.7 + 0.79 + 3.25 =$ _____   **30.** $4{,}876 - 2{,}523 =$ _____

31. $50.04 - 12.39 =$ _____   **32.** $243.44 \div 2.72 =$ _____   **33.** $141.52 \times 12.6 \div 305.2 =$ _____

Use mental computation to add, subtract, multiply, or divide.

34. $593 + 110 =$ _____   **35.** $\$215 + \$190 =$ _____   **36.** $8.05 + 7.29 =$ _____

37. $33 - 17 =$ _____   **38.** $\$3.00 - \$0.58 =$ _____   **39.** $100 \times 41 =$ _____

40. $58.9 \div 10 =$ _____   **41.** $0.0113 \times 1{,}000 =$ _____   **42.** $29.06 \div 10 =$ _____

Estimate.

43. $865 + 796 \approx$ _____   **44.** $614 - 398 \approx$ _____   **45.** $\$2.86 + \$7.52 \approx$ _____

46. $3.35 - 1.45 \approx$ _____   **47.** $52 \times 78 \approx$ _____   **48.** $52.8 \div 7.5 \approx$ _____

Estimate to choose the reasonable answer.

49. $76 + 74.9 + 365.2 \approx$ _____   **a.** 5.2   **b.** 520   **c.** 5,200

50. $5{,}260 \div 19 \approx$ _____   **a.** 2.768   **b.** 27.68   **c.** 276.8

Solve.

51. Kyle's birthday is on Saturday, and his friends are throwing him a surprise party. The total bill was $118. Eight of Kyle's friends split the cost. How much was each person's equal share of the bill?

_____

52. Tomato sauce costs 98¢ per can, noodles cost $1.75 per package, grated cheese costs $2.15 per container, and baseball cards cost $2 per pack. If Thomas needs five cans of sauce, two packages of noodles, and one container of cheese, how many packs of cards can Thomas buy if he has $15?

_____

53. Sue is cutting pieces of ribbon $8\frac{1}{8}$ inches long. About how many pieces can she cut from a 10-foot length of ribbon? _____

Part II:
Taxes

Pre-Skills Test

Add.

1. $329 + $981+ $523.18 = _____

2. $1,089 + $104 + $161 = _____

3. $4,092.67 + $234.81 + $3,009.61 = _____

4. $2,068.41 + $90.38 + $18.42 = _____

5. $109.57 + $1,037.62 + $73.56 = _____

6. $32,087 + $56.78 + $345.91 = _____

Subtract.

7. $947 − $186 = _____

8. $2,098 − $1,076 = _____

9. $372.41 − $186.37 = _____

10. $2,376.51 − $1,341.29 = _____

11. $913.07 − $568.71 = _____

12. $3,076.41 − $1,356.78 = _____

Rename as a decimal.

13. 2% _____

14. 5% _____

15. 3.5% _____

16. 6.5% _____

17. 7.5% _____

18. 2.75% _____

Multiply. Round to the nearest cent.

19. $0.02 \times $5,000 = _____

20. $0.05 \times $3,000 = _____

21. $0.075 \times $7,000 = _____

22. $0.05 \times $486.34 = _____

23. $0.065 \times $4,520.38 = _____

24. $0.035 \times $28,962.41 = _____

37

Name _____ Date _____

Find the answer.

25. 2% of $8,500 _____

26. 2.75% of $19,500 _____

27. 7.5% of $28,762.41 _____

Use the Taxable Income table. In which interval does the taxable income lie?

Taxable Income

If line 43 (taxable income) is —			
At least	But less than	At least	But less than
23,000		**31,000**	
23,000	23,050	31,000	31,050
23,050	23,100	31,050	31,100
23,100	23,150	31,100	31,150
23,150	23,200	31,150	31,200
23,200	23,250	31,200	31,250
23,250	23,300	31,250	31,300
23,300	23,350	31,300	13,350
23,350	23,400	31,350	31,400
23,400	23,450	31,400	31,450
23,450	23,500	31,450	31,500
23,500	23,550	31,500	31,550
23,550	23,600	31,550	31,600
23,600	23,650	31,600	31,650
23,650	23,700	31,650	31,700
23,700	23,750	31,700	31,750
23,750	23,800	31,750	31,800
23,800	23,850	31,800	31,850
23,850	23,900	31,850	31,900
23,900	23,950	31,900	31,950
23,950	24,000	31,950	32,000

28. $23,888 _____

29. $23,800 _____

30. $31,917 _____

31. $31,033 _____

32. $31,459 _____

33. $23,617 _____

34. $23,258 _____

35. $31,070 _____

Name _____   Date _____

Reporting Income

In 2009, you worked at Namca Industries. At the end of the year, the company sent you a **W-2 form**. The form shows how much you earned and how much was withheld for federal taxes, Social Security, and state and local taxes. The company sent copies of the W-2 form to federal and local tax agencies.

Example 1: Read and interpret this W-2 form.

Earnings

Federal Income Tax Withheld

Social Security Withheld

22222	a Employee's social security number	OMB No. 1545-0008

b Employer identification number (EIN)	1 Wages, tips, other compensation 34335.97	2 Federal income tax withheld 4835.35
c Employer's name, address, and ZIP code 38970	3 Social security wages 34335.97	4 Social security tax withheld 2128.83
	5 Medicare wages and tips 34335.97	6 Medicare tax withheld 497.87
Namca Industries	7 Social security tips	8 Allocated tips

d Control number — 9 Advance EIC payment — 10 Dependent care benefits

e Employee's first name and initial   Last name   Suff.
11 Nonqualified plans
12a
13 Statutory employee / Retirement plan [X] / Third-party sick pay
12b
14 Other
12c

(your name & address)

12d

f Employee's address and ZIP code

15 State Employer's state ID number	16 State wages, tips, etc.	17 State income tax	18 Local wages, tips, etc.	19 Local income tax	20 Locality name

Form **W-2** Wage and Tax Statement
Copy 1—For State, City, or Local Tax Department

2009

Department of the Treasury—Internal Revenue Service

State   (None)   Local

In 2009, you also earned interest from your bank account. The bank sent a **1099 form** to show how much interest you earned.

Example 2: Read and interpret this 1099 form.

Interest Income

2009 FORM 1099-INT: INTEREST INCOME

Account Type	Account Number	Deposit Number	Deposit ID	IRS Description	IRS Box	# Amount
NOW Account				Interest Income	1	71.62
Savings				Interest Income	1	2.90
TOTALS:	Interest Income				1	74.52
	Early withdrawal penalty				2	0.00
	Interest on U.S. Savings Bonds and Treasury obligations				3	0.00
	Federal income tax withheld				4	0.00
	Investment expenses				5	0.00
	Foreign tax paid				6	0.00
	Tax-exempt interest				8	0.00
	Specified private activity bond interest				9	0.00

Taxpayer I.D. NO.

Department of the Treasury - Internal Revue Service

Your **gross income** is the total of earnings, interest, and dividends.

Example 3: What was your gross income last year?

Add. $34,335.97 + $74.52 = $34,410.49

Think About It

1. Why are copies of the W-2 and 1099 forms sent to federal, state, and local tax agencies?

_____

_____

2. How could you check your W-2 form to be sure it is correct?

_____

_____

Practice

Use the W-2 form on page 39 for Exercises 1–4. How much was withheld for:

1. Federal income tax? _____

2. Social Security tax? _____

3. State income tax? _____

4. Local income tax? _____

Find the gross income.

5. Wages: $37,400
   Interest: $450

   Income: _____

6. Wages: $48,950
   Interest: $310

   Income: _____

7. Wages: $66,320
   Interest: $887

   Income: _____

8. Wages: $70,000
   Interest: $945

   Income: _____

9. Wages: $82,366
   Interest: $883

   Income: _____

10. Wages: $25,690
    Interest: $20

    Income: _____

The Mathematics of Housing and Taxes, SV 9780547625645

Name _____   Date _____

Remember to estimate whenever you use your calculator.
Find the gross income.

11. Wages: $18,359
Interest: $362

_____

12. Wages: $31,961
Interest: $965

_____

13. Wages: $21,029
Interest: $302

_____

14. Wages: $39, 224
Wages: $43,236
Interest: 871

_____

15. Wages: $59,002
Interest $1,030

_____

16. Wages: $19, 488
Tips: $15,780
Interest: $495

_____

17. Wages: $59,708
Interest: $1,804
Interest: $495

_____

18. Wages: $27,002
Interest: $876

_____

19. Wages: $79,828
Interest: $1,804
Interest: $595

_____

20. Wages: $25,870
Tips: $11, 973
Interest: $379

_____

21. Wages: $19,900
Tips: $2,220
Tips: $456
Interest: $625.33
Interest: $104.17

_____

22. Wages: $13,570
Wages: $15,345
Interest: $231.76
Interest: $197.33

_____

23. Wages: $12,85
Wages: $42,789
Interest: $102.26
Interest: $78.39

_____

24. Wages: $19,345
Wages: $14,597
Tips: $8,712
Tips: $1,588
Interest: $375.75
Interest: 83.34

_____

25. Wages: $24,118
Wages: $12,660
Tips: $10,187
Interest: $762.56
Interest: $92.93

_____

The Mathematics of Housing and Taxes, SV 9780547625645

Name _____ Date _____

Use Rosa Morales' W-2 and 1099 forms for Exercises 1–6.

22222	**a** Employee's social security number	OMB No. 1545-0008		
b Employer identification number (EIN)		**1** Wages, tips, other compensation 21,972.00	**2** Federal income tax withheld 3,295.80	
c Employer's name, address, and ZIP code DENMCO Industries		**3** Social security wages 21,972.00	**4** Social security tax withheld 1,648.90	
		5 Medicare wages and tips	**6** Medicare tax withheld	
		7 Social security tips	**8** Allocated tips	
d Control number		**9** Advance EIC payment	**10** Dependent care benefits	
e Employee's first name and initial Last name Suff.		**11** Nonqualified plans	**12a**	
		13 Statutory employee / Retirement plan / Third-party sick pay	**12b**	
Rosa Morales 1285 Riviera Drive Tucson, AZ 85832		**14** Other	**12c**	
			12d	
f Employee's address and ZIP code				

15 State Employer's state ID number	**16** State wages, tips, etc.	**17** State income tax	**18** Local wages, tips, etc.	**19** Local income tax	**20** Locality name
AZ	21,972.00	472.40	21,972.00	164.79	Tucson

Form **W-2** Wage and Tax Statement

Copy 1—For State, City, or Local Tax Department

2009

Department of the Treasury—Internal Revenue Service

☐ CORRECTED (if checked)

PAYER'S name, street address, city, state, ZIP code, and telephone no. VILLAGE BANK	Payer's RTN (optional)	OMB No. 1545-0112	**Interest Income**
	1 Interest income $ 315.26	**20**11	
	2 Early withdrawal penalty $	Form **1099-INT**	
PAYER'S federal identification number	RECIPIENT'S identification number 000-00-0000	**3** Interest on U.S. Savings Bonds and Treas. obligations $	**Copy B** **For Recipient**
RECIPIENT'S name Rosa Morales		**4** Federal income tax withheld $	**5** Investment expenses $
Street address (including apt. no.) 1285 Riviera Drive		**6** Foreign tax paid $	**7** Foreign country or U.S. possession
City, state, and ZIP code Tucson, AZ 85832		**8** Tax-exempt interest $	**9** Specified private activity bond interest $
Account number (see instructions)		**10** Tax-exempt bond CUSIP no. (see instructions)	

This is important tax information and is being furnished to the Internal Revenue Service. If you are required to file a return, a negligence penalty or other sanction may be imposed on you if this income is taxable and the IRS determines that it has not been reported.

Form **1099-INT**   (keep for your records)   Department of the Treasury - Internal Revenue Service

26. Wages _____

27. Federal income tax withheld _____

28. Social Security tax withheld _____

29. State tax withheld _____

30. Local tax withheld _____

31. Interest income _____

Federal Income Taxes

The **Internal Revenue Service (IRS)** collects **federal income taxes**. Tax receipts are used primarily for social and defense programs, and to pay interest on the national debt.

Tax deductions and **tax exemptions** reduce the amounts of income to be taxed. **Adjusted Gross Income (AGI)** is gross income less any adjustments to income. **Taxable income** is AGI less any exemptions or deductions. Your federal taxes are based on your taxable income.

Example 1: Last year, your gross income was $42,021.45. You had no adjustments to income and you are entitled to 1 exemption of $3,650. You had a standard deduction of $5,700. What is your AGI and your taxable income?

THINK: There were no adjustments. Your Adjusted Gross Income (AGI) is the same as your gross income.

| Step 1 | Add to find the total of exemptions and deductions. | $3,650 + $5,700 = $9,350. |

| Step 2 | Subtract to find your taxable income. | $42,021.45 – $9,350 = $32,671.45. |

Your taxable income is $35,671.45.

You use tax tables to find the tax due. You use your **filing status to find your tax**.

Example 2: If you are single, how much tax do you owe on $5,611?

THINK: Find your taxable income in the table. $5,611 is between $5,600 and $5,650.

Look down the "Single" column to find your tax.

Your tax is $563.

If line 43 (taxable income) is—		And you are—			
At least	But less than	Single	Married filing jointly *	Married filing sepa-rately	Head of a house-hold
				Your tax is—	
5,000					
5,000	5,050	503	503	503	503
5,050	5,100	508	508	508	508
5,100	5,150	513	513	513	513
5,150	5,200	518	518	518	518
5,200	5,250	523	523	523	523
5,250	5,300	528	528	528	528
5,300	5,350	533	533	533	533
5,350	5,400	538	538	538	538
5,400	5,450	543	543	543	543
5,450	5,500	548	548	548	548
5,500	5,550	553	553	553	553
5,550	5,600	558	558	558	558
5,600	5,650	563	563	563	563
5,650	5,700	568	568	568	568
5,700	5,750	573	573	573	573
5,750	5,800	578	578	578	578
5,800	5,850	583	583	583	583
5,850	5,900	588	588	588	588
5,900	5,950	593	593	593	593
5,950	6,000	598	598	598	598

The Mathematics of Housing and Taxes, SV 9780547625645

If too much tax was withheld, you will get a **refund**. If not enough tax was withheld, you will owe more taxes.

Example 3: You had $6,605 withheld in federal taxes. Your federal tax is actually $6,925. How much do you owe or how much of a refund can you expect?

THINK: The tax withheld is less than the tax. You will owe money.

Subtract. $6,925 − $6,605 = $320

You will owe $320.

STANDARD DEDUCTIONS	
Single or married, filing separately	$5,700
Married, filing jointly or qualifying widow(er):	$11,400
Head of household:	$8,400

FEDERAL EXEMPTIONS	
Individual	$3,650
Married, filing jointly:	$3,650 apiece (unless either is claimed on someone else's tax return)

Think About It

1. How can 2 people with the same taxable income pay different taxes?

_____

_____

_____

Practice

Remember to estimate whenever you use your calculator.

Find the Adjusted Gross Income (AGI) and taxable income.

1. Gross income: $40,876
   Adjustments: $1,500
   1 Exemption: $3,650
   Deduction: $5,700

   AGI = _____

   Taxable income = _____

2. Gross income: $120,000
   Adjustments: $25,328
   2 Exemptions: $7,300
   Deduction: $14,350

   AGI = _____

   Taxable income = _____

How much tax is owed or how much of a refund can be expected?

3. Tax withheld: $2,110.35
   Actual tax: $2,407

   _____

4. Tax withheld: $5,817.89
   Actual tax: $4,829

   _____

5. Tax withheld: $8,324.13
   Actual tax: $7,899

   _____

6. Tax withheld: $4,976.54
   Actual tax: $5,080

   _____

Name _____ Date _____

Use the chart to answer the following questions.

How much tax does a married person, filing jointly, owe on the following amounts?

7. $12,050 _____

8. $12,566 _____

9. $12,701 _____

Married, filing separately?

10. $12,777 _____

11. $12,905 _____

12. $12,950 _____

Head of household?

13. $13,001 _____

14. $13,200 _____

15. $13,551 _____

Single?

16. $13,649 _____

17. $13,749 _____

18. $13,953 _____

If line 43 (taxable income) is—		And you are—			
At least	But less than	Single	Married filing jointly *	Married filing separately	Head of a household
		Your tax is—			
12,000					
12,000	12,050	1,385	1,203	1,385	1,206
12,050	12,100	1,393	1,208	1,393	1,214
12,100	12,150	1,400	1,213	1,400	1,221
12,150	12,200	1,408	1,218	1,408	1,229
12,200	12,250	1,415	1,223	1,415	1,236
12,250	12,300	1,423	1,228	1,423	1,244
12,300	12,350	1,430	1,233	1,430	1,251
12,350	12,400	1,438	1,238	1,438	1,259
12,400	12,450	1,445	1,243	1,445	1,266
12,450	12,500	1,453	1,248	1,453	1,274
12,500	12,550	1,460	1,253	1,460	1,281
12,550	12,600	1,468	1,258	1,468	1,289
12,600	12,650	1,475	1,263	1,475	1,296
12,650	12,700	1,483	1,268	1,483	1,304
12,700	12,750	1,490	1,273	1,490	1,311
12,750	12,800	1,498	1,278	1,498	1,319
12,800	12,850	1,505	1,283	1,505	1,326
12,850	12,900	1,513	1,288	1,513	1,334
12,900	12,950	1,520	1,293	1,520	1,341
12,950	13,000	1,528	1,298	1,528	1,349
13,000					
13,000	13,050	1,535	1,303	1,535	1,356
13,050	13,100	1,543	1,308	1,543	1,364
13,100	13,150	1,550	1,313	1,550	1,371
13,150	13,200	1,558	1,318	1,558	1,379
13,200	13,250	1,565	1,323	1,565	1,386
13,250	13,300	1,573	1,328	1,573	1,394
13,300	13,350	1,580	1,333	1,580	1,401
13,350	13,400	1,588	1,338	1,588	1,409
13,400	13,450	1,595	1,343	1,595	1,416
13,450	13,500	1,603	1,348	1,603	1,424
13,500	13,550	1,610	1,353	1,610	1,431
13,550	13,600	1,618	1,358	1,618	1,439
13,600	13,650	1,625	1,363	1,625	1,446
13,650	13,700	1,633	1,368	1,633	1,454
13,700	13,750	1,640	1,373	1,640	1,461
13,750	13,800	1,648	1,378	1,648	1,469
13,800	13,850	1,655	1,383	1,655	1,476
13,850	13,900	1,663	1,388	1,663	1,484
13,900	13,950	1,670	1,393	1,670	1,491
13,950	14,000	1,678	1,398	1,678	1,499

Part II
The Mathematics of Housing and Taxes, SV 9780547625645

Name _____ Date _____

Use the tax tables on pp. 139–145 of this book. Find the adjusted gross income, the taxable income, and the amount owed.

19. Single
Gross income: $25,374
Adjustments: $750
Exemptions: $3,650
Deduction: $5,700

AGI = _____

Taxable income = _____

Tax (from chart) = _____

20. Married, filing separately
Gross income: $83,092
Adjustments: $3,762
Exemptions: $3,650
Deduction: $10,075

AGI = _____

Taxable income = _____

Tax (from chart) = _____

21. Single
Gross income: $75,629
Adjustments: $8,305
Exemption: $3,650
Deduction: $6,215

AGI = _____

Taxable income = _____

Tax (from chart) = _____

22. Married, filing jointly
Gross income: $60,926
Adjustments: $1,500
Exemptions: $7,500
Deduction: $6,550

AGI = _____

Taxable income = _____

Tax (from chart) = _____

23. Married, filing separately
Gross income: $65,000
Adjustments: $0
Exemption: $3,650
Deduction: $7,175

AGI = _____

Taxable income = _____

Tax (from chart) = _____

24. Head of Household, under 65
Gross income: $92,550
Adjustments: $10,217
Exemptions: $14,600
Deduction: $12,897

AGI = _____

Taxable income = _____

Tax (from chart) = _____

25. Married, filing jointly
Gross income: $80,211
Adjustments: $2,750
Exemption: $0
Deduction: $14,206

AGI = _____

Taxable income = _____

Tax (from chart) = _____

26. Single Head/household, over 65
Gross income: $56,872
Adjustments: $0
Exemptions: $7,300
Deduction: $9,800

AGI = _____

Taxable income = _____

Tax (from chart) = _____

Name _____ Date _____

Problem Solving Application: Federal Income Taxes

The IRS provides **tax rate schedules** so you can see the tax rate that applies to all levels of taxable income. This is used to give you an idea of how your federal tax is computed.

2010 Tax Rate Schedules

The Tax Rate Schedules are shown so you can see the tax rate that applies to all levels of taxable income. Do not use them to figure your tax. Instead, see the instructions for line 44 on page 35.

Schedule X—If your filing status is Single

If your taxable income is:		The tax is:	of the amount over—
Over—	But not over—		
$0	$8,375	········· 10%	$0
8,375	34,000	$837.50 + 15%	8,375
34,000	82,400	4,681.25 + 25%	34,000
82,400	171,850	16,781.25 + 28%	82,400
171,850	373,650	41,827.25 + 33%	171,850
373,650	·········	108,421.25 + 35%	373,650

Example: Marcie Graham is single and her taxable income is $43,250. During the year, she had $6,487.50 withheld from her paychecks. How much in additional taxes does Marcie need to pay?

Step 1 Read the instructions under 'Schedule X'—the one for single people.

THINK: $43,250 is greater than $34,000 and less than $82,400.

Step 2 Find the total tax.

(a) Subtract to find out how much greater $43,250 is than $34,000.

$$\$43,250 - \$34,000 = \$9,250$$

(b) Multiply to find 25% of $9,250. THINK: 25% = 0.25

$$0.25 \times \$9,250 = \$2,312.50$$

(c) Add to find the total tax.

$$\$2,312.50 + \$4,681.25 = \$6,993.75$$

Recall: Marcie only had $6,487.50 withheld, so she will have to pay.

Step 3 Subtract to find the amount owed.
$$\$6,993.75 - \$6,487.50 = \$506.25$$

So, Marcie needs to pay $506.25 in additional taxes.

Name _____ Date _____

Use the table on page 47. Find the federal income tax for a single taxpayer. (Remember to estimate whenever you use your calculator.)

Taxable income	Federal Income Tax
$8,000	1. $ _____
$8,950	2. $ _____
$20,500	3. $ _____
$26,872	4. $ _____
$34,875	5. $ _____
$62,500	6. $ _____
$82,950	7. $ _____
$96,780	8. $ _____
$171,000	9. $ _____
$223,600	10. $ _____
$375,000	11. $ _____
$450,960	12. $ _____

Find the tax for a taxpayer filing as "single." Then determine whether an amount is still owed or is to be refunded.

Taxable income	Federal Income tax	Amount withheld	Amount owed	Amount of refund
$6,575	13. $ _____	$856	14. $ _____	15. $ _____
$43,100	16. $ _____	$6,500	17. $ _____	18. $ _____
$55,930	19. $ _____	$8,389.50	20. $ _____	21. $ _____
$108,426	22. $ _____	$25,000	23. $ _____	24. $ _____

The Mathematics of Housing and Taxes, SV 9780547625645

Name _____   Date _____

Sonny Lacroix and his wife Magdalena file their income taxes separately each year. Answer the following questions about their situation.

Schedule Y-1—If your filing status is **Married filing jointly** or **Qualifying widow(er)**

If your taxable income is:		The tax is:	of the amount over—
Over—	But not over—		
$0	$16,750	.... 10%	$0
16,750	68,000	$1,675.00 + 15%	16,750
68,000	137,300	9,362.50 + 25%	68,000
137,300	209,250	26,687.50 + 28%	137,300
209,250	373,650	46,833.50 + 33%	209,250
373,650	....	101,085.50 + 35%	373,650

Schedule Y-2—If your filing status is **Married filing separately**

If your taxable income is:		The tax is:	of the amount over—
Over—	But not over—		
$0	$8,375	.... 10%	$0
8,375	34,000	$837.50 + 15%	8,375
34,000	68,650	4,681.25 + 25%	34,000
68,650	104,625	13,343.75 + 28%	68,650
104,625	186,825	23,416.75 + 33%	104,625
186,825	....	50,542.75 + 35%	186,825

25. Sonny's taxable income was $52,570 last year. According to Schedule Y-2, what is the amount of his federal income tax?

_____

26. Magdalena's taxable income was $69,500 last year. As a married person filing taxes separately from her spouse, how much are her federal income taxes?

_____

27. Look at Schedules Y-1, Y-2, and X (which is on page 47). Assuming she made the same amount last year, what would Magdalena's taxes have been if she were

(a) single _____

(b) married, filing jointly? _____

If she were single, Magdalena would have paid (c)$ _____ {less, more} in taxes last year.

If Magdalena and Sonny had filed their taxes jointly, Magdalena would have paid (d) $ _____ {less, more} in taxes last year.

Use Schedules Y-1 and Y-2 on page 49 to answer the following questions.

28. What is the federal tax obligation for a couple filing jointly whose taxable income is $372,000?

_____

29. If Bob and Mary Martindale file separately, how much will Bob be taxed on the $98,750 in taxable income he made last year?

_____

30. John Sanger and his wife, Sue, filed their taxes jointly last year. Together, their taxable income was $68,000. How much are their taxes?

_____

31. The Samuelsons earned $68,101 last year and filed their taxes jointly. What was their tax obligation?

_____

32. Ross earned $68,775 in taxable income last year and filed taxes separately from his wife, Shari. What did he owe in taxes?

_____

The Mathematics of Housing and Taxes, SV 9780547625645

Using Tax Form 1040EZ

Tax Form 1040EZ is often called the **short form**. This form can only be used if your filing status is single and you have no dependents. You can use the information from the W-2 and 1099 forms to complete Form 1040EZ.

22222	**a** Employee's social security number			
	OMB No. 1545-0008			
b Employer identification number (EIN)		**1** Wages, tips, other compensation 21,050.37	**2** Federal income tax withheld 1,581.31	
c Employer's name, address, and ZIP code		**3** Social security wages	**4** Social security tax withheld 1,496.31	
		5 Medicare wages and tips	**6** Medicare tax withheld	
		7 Social security tips	**8** Allocated tips	
d Control number		**9** Advance EIC payment	**10** Dependent care benefits	
e Employee's first name and initial Last name Suff.		**11** Nonqualified plans	**12a**	
		13 Statutory employee Retirement plan Third-party sick pay	**12b**	
Chad Blair		**14** Other	**12c**	
			12d	
f Employee's address and ZIP code				
15 State Employer's state ID number	**16** State wages, tips, etc.	**17** State income tax 475.43	**18** Local wages, tips, etc.	**19** Local income tax 120.90	**20** Locality name

Form **W-2** **Wage and Tax Statement**   2009   Department of the Treasury—Internal Revenue Service
Copy 1—For State, City, or Local Tax Department

		CORRECTED (if checked)	
PAYER'S name, street address, city, state, ZIP code, and telephone no.	Payer's RTN (optional)	OMB No. 1545-0112	
	1 Interest income $ 241.68	2011	**Interest Income**
	2 Early withdrawal penalty $	Form **1099-INT**	
PAYER'S federal identification number RECIPIENT'S identification number	**3** Interest on U.S. Savings Bonds and Treas. obligations $		**Copy B For Recipient**
RECIPIENT'S name Chad Blair	**4** Federal income tax withheld $	**5** Investment expenses $	This is important tax information and is being furnished to the Internal Revenue Service. If you are required to file a return, a
Street address (including apt. no.)	**6** Foreign tax paid $	**7** Foreign country or U.S. possession	negligence penalty or other sanction may be imposed on you if this income is
City, state, and ZIP code	**8** Tax-exempt interest $	**9** Specified private activity bond interest $	taxable and the IRS determines that it has not been reported.
Account number (see instructions)	**10** Tax-exempt bond CUSIP no. (see instructions)		

Form **1099-INT**   (keep for your records)   Department of the Treasury - Internal Revenue Service

To complete his federal income tax form Chad needs the following information from his W-2 and his 1099 (interest income) forms:

1. Wages, tips, and other compensation (all jobs)

2. Interest income

3. Federal income tax withheld

Also, he will have to consult a tax table like the one shown on page 53.

Name _____ Date _____

Read and interpret Chad Blaire's tax form 1040EZ:

Department of the Treasury—Internal Revenue Service

Form 1040EZ

Income Tax Return for Single and Joint Filers With No Dependents (99) **2010**

OMB No. 1545-0074

Name, Address, and SSN

See separate instructions.

P R I N T   C L E A R L Y

Your first name and initial	Last name	Your social security number
Chad	Blair	000 00 0000

If a joint return, spouse's first name and initial	Last name	Spouse's social security number

Home address (number and street). If you have a P.O. box, see instructions.   Apt. no.
33 Robin Lane

▲ Make sure the SSN(s) above are correct. ▲

City, town or post office, state, and ZIP code. If you have a foreign address, see instructions.
Hometown, USA 00000

Checking a box below will not change your tax or refund.

Presidential Election Campaign (see page 9) ▶

Check here if you, or your spouse if a joint return, want $3 to go to this fund . . ▶ ☒ **You**   ☐ **Spouse**

Income

Attach Form(s) W-2 here.

Enclose, but do not attach, any payment.

> You may be entitled to a larger deduction if you file Form 1040A or 1040. See *Before You Begin* on page 4.

1	Wages, salaries, and tips. This should be shown in box 1 of your Form(s) W-2. Attach your Form(s) W-2.	1	21,050 37
2	Taxable interest. If the total is over $1,500, you cannot use Form 1040EZ.	2	241 68
3	Unemployment compensation and Alaska Permanent Fund dividends (see page 11).	3	0 00
4	Add lines 1, 2, and 3. This is your **adjusted gross income.**	4	21,292 05
5	If someone can claim you (or your spouse if a joint return) as a dependent, check the applicable box(es) below and enter the amount from the worksheet on back. ☐ **You** ☐ **Spouse** If no one can claim you (or your spouse if a joint return), enter $9,350 if **single;** $18,700 if **married filing jointly.** See back for explanation.	5	9,350 00
6	Subtract line 5 from line 4. If line 5 is larger than line 4, enter -0-. This is your **taxable income.** ▶	6	11,942 05

Payments, Credits, and Tax

7	Federal income tax withheld from Form(s) W-2 and 1099.	7	1,581 31
8	Making work pay credit (see worksheet on back).	8	0 00
9a	**Earned income credit (EIC)** (see page 13).	9a	0 00
b	Nontaxable combat pay election. 9b		
10	Add lines 7, 8, and 9a. These are your **total payments and credits.** ▶	10	1,581 31
11	**Tax.** Use the amount on **line 6 above** to find your tax in the tax table on pages 27 through 35 of the instructions. Then, enter the tax from the table on this line.	11	1,370 00

Refund

Have it directly deposited! See page 18 and fill in 12b, 12c, and 12d or Form 8888.

12a	If line 10 is larger than line 11, subtract line 11 from line 10. This is your **refund.** If Form 8888 is attached, check here ▶ ☐	12a	211 31
▶ b	Routing number	▶ c Type: ☐ Checking ☐ Savings	
▶ d	Account number		

Amount You Owe

13	If line 11 is larger than line 10, subtract line 10 from line 11. This is the **amount you owe.** For details on how to pay, see page 19. ▶	13	

Third Party Designee

Do you want to allow another person to discuss this return with the IRS (see page 20)? ☐ **Yes.** Complete the following. ☐ **No**

Designee's name ▶ _____ Phone no. ▶ _____ Personal identification number (PIN) ▶ _____

Sign Here

Under penalties of perjury, I declare that I have examined this return, and to the best of my knowledge and belief, it is true, correct, and accurately lists all amounts and sources of income I received during the tax year. Declaration of preparer (other than the taxpayer) is based on all information of which the preparer has any knowledge.

Joint return? See page 6.

Keep a copy for your records.

Your signature	Date	Your occupation	Daytime phone number
Chad Blair	4/12/11	cashier	
Spouse's signature. If a joint return, **both** must sign.	Date	Spouse's occupation	

Paid Preparer Use Only

Print/Type preparer's name	Preparer's signature	Date	Check ☐ if self-employed	PTIN
Firm's name ▶			Firm's EIN ▶	
Firm's address ▶			Phone no.	

For Disclosure, Privacy Act, and Paperwork Reduction Act Notice, see page 36.   Cat. No. 11329W   Form **1040EZ** (2010)

How to complete Form 1040EZ:

- Chad entered his name, address, and Social Security number. The form cannot be processed without the Social Security number.

- The IRS would prefer that you e-file your taxes. As they say at their website, you get your refund faster, if you are owed one.

If line 43 (taxable income) is—		And you are—			
At least	But less than	Single	Married filing jointly *	Married filing sepa-rately	Head of a house-hold
		Your tax is—			
11,000					
11,000	11,050	1,235	1,103	1,235	1,103
11,050	11,100	1,243	1,108	1,243	1,108
11,100	11,150	1,250	1,113	1,250	1,113
11,150	11,200	1,258	1,118	1,258	1,118
11,200	11,250	1,265	1,123	1,265	1,123
11,250	11,300	1,273	1,128	1,273	1,128
11,300	11,350	1,280	1,133	1,280	1,133
11,350	11,400	1,288	1,138	1,288	1,138
11,400	11,450	1,295	1,143	1,295	1,143
11,450	11,500	1,303	1,148	1,303	1,148
11,500	11,550	1,310	1,153	1,310	1,153
11,550	11,600	1,318	1,158	1,318	1,158
11,600	11,650	1,325	1,163	1,325	1,163
11,650	11,700	1,333	1,168	1,333	1,168
11,700	11,750	1,340	1,173	1,340	1,173
11,750	11,800	1,348	1,178	1,348	1,178
11,800	11,850	1,355	1,183	1,355	1,183
11,850	11,900	1,363	1,188	1,363	1,188
11,900	11,950	1,370	1,193	1,370	1,193
11,950	12,000	1,378	1,198	1,378	1,199

Line 1   Remember to attach a copy of your W-2 form(s) if you are completing the form by hand instead of electronically. You must report earnings even if you don't get a W-2 form.

Line 2   Do not attach a copy of Form 1099. Do not use form 1040EZ if your interest income is over $1,500.

Line 5   Chad is entitled to the standard deduction.

Line 7   Chad used information from his W-2 form to enter the tax withheld.

Line 11   Chad used the amount from Line 6 to find his tax in the tax table. His taxable income falls between $11,900 and $11,950. He finds his tax in the tax table for single persons.

Line 12a   If Chad is due a refund, the IRS will mail him a check a few weeks after his tax form is processed. If he files online, he can indicate a bank account for deposit of his refund.

Line 13   If Chad still owed money to the IRS, he could enclose a check, or he could arrange to pay online or by phone.

Practice

Remember to estimate whenever you use your calculator.
Use Chad Blair's Form 1040EZ for Exercises 1–6.

1. What is Chad's gross income? _____

2. What is Chad's AGI? _____

3. What is Chad's taxable income? _____

4. How much federal tax was withheld? _____

5. What is Chad's federal tax? _____

6. How much is Chad's refund? _____

The Mathematics of Housing and Taxes, SV 9780547625645

Name _____ Date _____

Below are copies of Stacey Lee's W-2 and 1099 forms. She is single and can't be claimed on another person's tax return.

Refer to Form 1040EZ on page 52 and the tax tables to the right to answer the following questions.

W-2 Form (2009)

22222	**a** Employee's social security number 000-00-0000	OMB No. 1545-0008

b Employer identification number (EIN)	**1** Wages, tips, other compensation 23,125.35	**2** Federal income tax withheld 3,558.00
c Employer's name, address, and ZIP code	**3** Social security wages	**4** Social security tax withheld 1,740.91
L&M Camping Supply	**5** Medicare wages and tips	**6** Medicare tax withheld
	7 Social security tips	**8** Allocated tips
d Control number	**9** Advance EIC payment	**10** Dependent care benefits
e Employee's first name and initial Last name Suff.	**11** Nonqualified plans	**12a**
	13 Statutory employee / Retirement plan / Third-party sick pay	**12b**
Stacey Lee	**14** Other	**12c**
		12d
f Employee's address and ZIP code		

15 State Employer's state ID number	**16** State wages, tips, etc. 23,125.35	**17** State income tax 718.16	**18** Local wages, tips, etc. 23,125.35	**19** Local income tax 83.82	**20** Locality name

Form **W-2** Wage and Tax Statement   **2009**   Department of the Treasury—Internal Revenue Service
Copy 1—For State, City, or Local Tax Department

1099-INT Form (2011)

☐ CORRECTED (if checked)

PAYER'S name, street address, city, state, ZIP code, and telephone no.	Payer's RTN (optional)	OMB No. 1545-0112
	1 Interest income $ 109.08	**2011** Interest Income
	2 Early withdrawal penalty $	Form **1099-INT**
PAYER'S federal identification number RECIPIENT'S identification number	**3** Interest on U.S. Savings Bonds and Treas. obligations $	**Copy B For Recipient**
RECIPIENT'S name Stacey Lee	**4** Federal income tax withheld $ **5** Investment expenses $	This is important tax information and is being furnished to the Internal Revenue Service. If you are required to file a return, a negligence penalty or other sanction may be imposed on you if this income is taxable and the IRS determines that it has not been reported.
Street address (including apt. no.)	**6** Foreign tax paid $ **7** Foreign country or U.S. possession	
City, state, and ZIP code	**8** Tax-exempt interest $ **9** Specified private activity bond interest $	
Account number (see instructions)	**10** Tax-exempt bond CUSIP no. (see instructions)	

Form **1099-INT**   (keep for your records)   Department of the Treasury - Internal Revenue Service

Tax Table

If line 43 (taxable income) is—		And you are—			
At least	But less than	Single	Married filing jointly *	Married filing separately	Head of a household
		Your tax is—			
12,000					
12,000	12,050	1,385	1,203	1,385	1,206
12,050	12,100	1,393	1,208	1,393	1,214
12,100	12,150	1,400	1,213	1,400	1,221
12,150	12,200	1,408	1,218	1,408	1,229
12,200	12,250	1,415	1,223	1,415	1,236
12,250	12,300	1,423	1,228	1,423	1,244
12,300	12,350	1,430	1,233	1,430	1,251
12,350	12,400	1,438	1,238	1,438	1,259
12,400	12,450	1,445	1,243	1,445	1,266
12,450	12,500	1,453	1,248	1,453	1,274
12,500	12,550	1,460	1,253	1,460	1,281
12,550	12,600	1,468	1,258	1,468	1,289
12,600	12,650	1,475	1,263	1,475	1,296
12,650	12,700	1,483	1,268	1,483	1,304
12,700	12,750	1,490	1,273	1,490	1,311
12,750	12,800	1,498	1,278	1,498	1,319
12,800	12,850	1,505	1,283	1,505	1,326
12,850	12,900	1,513	1,288	1,513	1,334
12,900	12,950	1,520	1,293	1,520	1,341
12,950	13,000	1,528	1,298	1,528	1,349
13,000					
13,000	13,050	1,535	1,303	1,535	1,356
13,050	13,100	1,543	1,308	1,543	1,364
13,100	13,150	1,550	1,313	1,550	1,371
13,150	13,200	1,558	1,318	1,558	1,379
13,200	13,250	1,565	1,323	1,565	1,386
13,250	13,300	1,573	1,328	1,573	1,394
13,300	13,350	1,580	1,333	1,580	1,401
13,350	13,400	1,588	1,338	1,588	1,409
13,400	13,450	1,595	1,343	1,595	1,416
13,450	13,500	1,603	1,348	1,603	1,424
13,500	13,550	1,610	1,353	1,610	1,431
13,550	13,600	1,618	1,358	1,618	1,439
13,600	13,650	1,625	1,363	1,625	1,446
13,650	13,700	1,633	1,368	1,633	1,454
13,700	13,750	1,640	1,373	1,640	1,461
13,750	13,800	1,648	1,378	1,648	1,469
13,800	13,850	1,655	1,383	1,655	1,476
13,850	13,900	1,663	1,388	1,663	1,484
13,900	13,950	1,670	1,393	1,670	1,491
13,950	14,000	1,678	1,398	1,678	1,499

To complete her 1040EZ form, what amount will Stacey put on:

7. Line 1? _____   **8.** Line 2? _____

9. Line 4? _____   **10.** Line 5? _____

11. Line 6? _____   **12.** Line 7? _____

13. Line 10? _____   **14.** Line 11? _____

15. Did Stacey get a refund, or did she owe taxes? _____

16. What was the amount she will either pay or receive? _____

Itemized Deductions

When you file your income tax return, you may have **itemized deductions** that would reduce your tax. Use Form 1040, Schedule A, to itemize deductions.

Example 1: Liz Ryan filed Form 1040 with Schedule A. Her Adjusted Gross Income (AGI) was $31,580 (on Form 1040, line 38). Read and interpret this Schedule A.

SCHEDULE A **(Form 1040)** Department of the Treasury Internal Revenue Service (99)	**Itemized Deductions** ▶ **Attach to Form 1040.** ▶ **See Instructions for Schedule A (Form 1040).**	OMB No. 1545-0074 20**10** Attachment Sequence No. **07**

Name(s) shown on Form 1040 | Your social security number
000 00 0000

Medical and Dental Expenses		**Caution.** Do not include expenses reimbursed or paid by others.		
	1	Medical and dental expenses (see instructions)	**1** *984 00*	
	2	Enter amount from Form 1040, line 38 **2** *31,580 00*		
	3	Multiply line 2 by 7.5% (.075)	**3** *2,369 00*	
	4	Subtract line 3 from line 1. If line 3 is more than line 1, enter -0-		**4** *0*

Taxes You Paid	5	State and local **(check only one box):**
		   a ☐ Income taxes, **or**
		   b ☐ General sales taxes
			5 *1,115 00*	

	6	Real estate taxes (see instructions)	**6** *1,163 00*	
	7	New motor vehicle taxes from line 11 of the worksheet on back (for certain vehicles purchased in 2009). Skip this line if you checked box 5b	**7**	
	8	Other taxes. List type and amount ▶ _____	**8**	
	9	Add lines 5 through 8		**9** *2,278 00*
Interest You Paid **Note.** Your mortgage interest deduction may be limited (see instructions).	10	Home mortgage interest and points reported to you on Form 1098	**10** *8,691 00*	
	11	Home mortgage interest not reported to you on Form 1098. If paid to the person from whom you bought the home, see instructions and show that person's name, identifying no., and address ▶ _____ _____	**11**	
	12	Points not reported to you on Form 1098. See instructions for special rules	**12**	
	13	Mortgage insurance premiums (see instructions)	**13**	
	14	Investment interest. Attach Form 4952 if required. (See instructions.)	**14**	
	15	Add lines 10 through 14		**15** *8,691 00*
Gifts to Charity If you made a gift and got a benefit for it, see instructions.	16	Gifts by cash or check. If you made any gift of $250 or more, see instructions	**16** *907 00*	
	17	Other than by cash or check. If any gift of $250 or more, see instructions. You **must** attach Form 8283 if over $500	**17** *75 00*	
	18	Carryover from prior year	**18**	
	19	Add lines 16 through 18		**19** *982 00*
Casualty and Theft Losses	20	Casualty or theft loss(es). Attach Form 4684. (See instructions.)	**20**	*0*
Job Expenses and Certain Miscellaneous Deductions	21	Unreimbursed employee expenses—job travel, union dues, job education, etc. Attach Form 2106 or 2106-EZ if required. (See instructions.) ▶ _____	**21** *683 00*	
	22	Tax preparation fees	**22**	
	23	Other expenses—investment, safe deposit box, etc. List type and amount ▶ _____	**23**	
	24	Add lines 21 through 23	**24** *683 00*	
	25	Enter amount from Form 1040, line 38 **25** *31,580 00*		
	26	Multiply line 25 by 2% (.02)	**26** *632 00*	
	27	Subtract line 26 from line 24. If line 26 is more than line 24, enter -0-	**27**	*51 00*
Other Miscellaneous Deductions	28	Other—from list in instructions. List type and amount ▶ _____	**28**	*0*
Total Itemized Deductions	29	Add the amounts in the far right column for lines 4 through 28. Also, enter this amount on Form 1040, line 40	**29**	*12,002 00*
	30	If you elect to itemize deductions even though they are less than your standard deduction, check here ▶ ☐		

For Paperwork Reduction Act Notice, see Form 1040 instructions.   Cat. No. 17145C   Schedule A (Form 1040) 2010

How to complete Schedule A—Itemized Deductions:

| Line 1 | Liz could not include health expenses paid for by insurance. |

| Line 3 | Liz multiplied 0.075 × $31,580 (the AGI) to get $2,369.00. She rounded to the nearest dollar to make computation easier. |

| Line 4 | Since Line 3 is greater than Line 1, Liz cannot take a deduction for medical and dental expenses. |

| Line 5 | These amounts are from Liz's W-2 form (not shown), plus any additional taxes she paid. Federal income taxes are not deductible. |

| Line 6 | Liz owns her house and pays real estate taxes. |

| Line 10 | The bank sent Liz a statement showing how much interest she had paid. (Not shown.) |

| Line 15 | This line shows the total deduction for interest. |

| Line 17 | This deduction is the value of books Liz donated to the library. |

| Line 19 | This line shows the total deduction for contributions. |

| Line 26 | Liz multiplied 0.02 × $31,580 to get $632. |

| Line 27 | Liz subtracted to find her total miscellaneous deductions. |

| Line 29 | This line shows the total of Liz's itemized deductions. |

Taxpayers who do not itemize their deductions may take a **standard deduction**. Only use itemized deductions if the total is more than the standard deduction. The amount of the standard deduction depends on filing status. Study the chart.

Example 2: Liz is single. Should she itemize deductions or use the standard deduction?

Liz compared the total of her itemized deductions ($12,002) with her standard deduction ($5,700). The total itemized deductions are greater than the standard deduction.

Liz will itemize deductions.

2010 Standard Deduction	
Married, Filing Jointly	$11,400
Single	$5,700
Married, Filing Separately	$5,700
Head of Household	$8,400
Blind or over 65 and married – add:	$1,100
Blind or over 65 and single/head of household – add:	$1,400

Name _____ Date _____

1. Why are homeowners likely to have more deductions than renters?

_____

_____

2. Why is it important to keep records of expenses you want to deduct on your tax return?

_____

_____

Practice

Remember to estimate whenever you use your calculator.
Use Liz Ryan's Schedule A on page 55 for problems 1–6.

1. What was Liz's deduction for real estate taxes? _____

2. What was Liz's deduction for contributions other than cash? _____

3. What was the total of Liz's unreimbursed business expenses? _____

4. How much of Liz's unreimbursed business expenses could be deducted? _____

5. What is the total of Liz's itemized deductions? _____

6. How much more than the standard deduction are Liz's itemized deductions? _____

Find the difference between the itemized and the standard deduction. Which should the person use?

7. Single
   Total itemized deductions: $5,380

   _____

8. Married, joint return
   Total itemized deductions: $10,256

   _____

9. Married, separate return
   Itemized deductions $6,952

   _____

10. Head of household
    Itemized deductions: $9,328

    _____

Name _____ Date _____

Find the total itemized deductions. Should the person(s) use the itemized or standard deduction? Use the blank Schedule A to assist you with your answers.

11. Lester Jefferson
Single
Adjusted Gross Income: $82,750
Allowable Medical Expenses (Line 1): $12,530
State and Local Taxes (Line 5): $240
Cash contributions (Line 16): $50
Casualty Loss (Line 20): $2,481

_____

12. Jim and Marge Cochran
Married, Filing a Joint Return
Adjusted Gross Income (Form 1040—Line 38): $67,500
Allowable Medical Expenses (Line 1): $8,306
Real Estate Taxes (Line 6): $4,780
Mortgage Interest (Line 10): $9,932.98
Cash contributions (Line 16): $200

_____

SCHEDULE A (Form 1040)	**Itemized Deductions**	OMB No. 1545-0074
Department of the Treasury Internal Revenue Service (99)	▶ Attach to Form 1040. ▶ See Instructions for Schedule A (Form 1040).	2010 Attachment Sequence No. 07

Name(s) shown on Form 1040   Your social security number

Medical and Dental Expenses	**Caution.** Do not include expenses reimbursed or paid by others.		
	1 Medical and dental expenses (see instructions)	1	
	2 Enter amount from Form 1040, line 38 |2|		
	3 Multiply line 2 by 7.5% (.075)	3	
	4 Subtract line 3 from line 1. If line 3 is more than line 1, enter -0-		4
Taxes You Paid	5 State and local (**check only one box**):		
	a ☐ Income taxes, **or**	5	
	b ☐ General sales taxes		
	6 Real estate taxes (see instructions)	6	
	7 New motor vehicle taxes from line 11 of the worksheet on back (for certain vehicles purchased in 2009). Skip this line if you checked box 5b	7	
	8 Other taxes. List type and amount ▶ _____		
		8	
	9 Add lines 5 through 8		9
Interest You Paid	10 Home mortgage interest and points reported to you on Form 1098	10	
	11 Home mortgage interest not reported to you on Form 1098. If paid to the person from whom you bought the home, see instructions and show that person's name, identifying no., and address ▶		
Note. Your mortgage interest deduction may be limited (see instructions).	_____	11	
	12 Points not reported to you on Form 1098. See instructions for special rules	12	
	13 Mortgage insurance premiums (see instructions)	13	
	14 Investment interest. Attach Form 4952 if required. (See instructions.)	14	
	15 Add lines 10 through 14		15
Gifts to Charity	16 Gifts by cash or check. If you made any gift of $250 or more, see instructions	16	
If you made a gift and got a benefit for it, see instructions.	17 Other than by cash or check. If any gift of $250 or more, see instructions. You **must** attach Form 8283 if over $500 . . .	17	
	18 Carryover from prior year	18	
	19 Add lines 16 through 18		19
Casualty and Theft Losses	20 Casualty or theft loss(es). Attach Form 4684. (See instructions.)		20
Job Expenses and Certain Miscellaneous Deductions	21 Unreimbursed employee expenses—job travel, union dues, job education, etc. Attach Form 2106 or 2106-EZ if required. (See instructions.) ▶ _____	21	
	22 Tax preparation fees	22	
	23 Other expenses—investment, safe deposit box, etc. List type and amount ▶ _____		
		23	
	24 Add lines 21 through 23	24	
	25 Enter amount from Form 1040, line 38 |25|		
	26 Multiply line 25 by 2% (.02)	26	
	27 Subtract line 26 from line 24. If line 26 is more than line 24, enter -0-		27
Other Miscellaneous Deductions	28 Other—from list in instructions. List type and amount ▶ _____		
			28
Total Itemized Deductions	29 Add the amounts in the far right column for lines 4 through 28. Also, enter this amount on Form 1040, line 40		29
	30 If you elect to itemize deductions even though they are less than your standard deduction, check here . . . . ▶ ☐		

For Paperwork Reduction Act Notice, see Form 1040 instructions. Cat. No. 17145C Schedule A (Form 1040) 2010

State and City Income Taxes

Some **state and city income taxes** are a percent of a person's Adjusted Gross Income from their federal tax Form 1040.

Example 1: Bob's AGI was $22,500. How much state tax does he owe?

STATE TAX	
Adjusted Gross Income	**Tax rate**
First $8,000	2%
Next $7,000	3.5%
Next $5,000	5%
Over $20,000	6.5%

Step 1 Multiply to find the tax.

First $8,000 $\rightarrow$ 0.02 $\times$ $8,000 = $160

Next $7,000 $\rightarrow$ 0.035 $\times$ $7,000 = $245

Next $5,000 $\rightarrow$ 0.05 $\times$ $5,000 = $250

Over $20,000 $\rightarrow$ 0.065 $\times$ $2,500 = $162.50

Step 2 Add to find the total tax. $817.50

Bob's state tax is $817.50.

Some states and cities have tax rates that include personal exemptions.

CITY EXEMPTIONS
Single: $1,750
Married: $3,400
Each dependent: $750

CITY TAX	
AGI	**Tax rate**
First $9,000	1.5%
Next $6,000	2.75%
Over $15,000	3.5%

Example 2: Kathy and Harry live in a small Midwestern town. They have a combined AGI of $29,540. They have one child. How much city income tax do they pay?

Step 1 Add to find their total exemption. $3,400 + $750 = $4,150

Step 2 Subtract to find the taxable income. $29,540 − $4,150 = $25,390

Step 3 Multiply to find the tax.

First $9,000 $\rightarrow$ 0.015 $\times$ $9,000 = $135

Next $6,000 $\rightarrow$ 0.0275 $\times$ $6,000 = $165

Over $15,000 $\rightarrow$ 0.035 $\times$ $10,390 = $363.65

Step 4 Add to find the total tax. $663.65

Kathy and Harry's tax is $663.65.

Part II
The Mathematics of Housing and Taxes, SV 9780547625645

Think About It

1. What taxes other than income taxes might a state or city have?

_____

_____

2. Why would a city or state need to raise money through income taxes?

_____

_____

Practice

Remember to estimate whenever you use your calculator.

Use the state tax table to find the state tax on the Adjusted Gross Income.

STATE TAX	
Adjusted Gross Income	**Tax rate**
First $8,000	2%
Next $7,000	3.5%
Next $5,000	5%
Over $20,000	6.5%

1. $6,872 _____

2. $13,581 _____

3. $20,615 _____

4. $19,762 _____

5. $43,181 _____

6. $12,924 _____

7. $7,240 _____

8. $19,783 _____

9. $16,195 _____

10. $28,526 _____

11. $10,637 _____

12. $35,449 _____

Use the city tax table and exemptions to find the city tax.

CITY EXEMPTIONS
Single: $1,750
Married: $3,400
Each dependent: $750

CITY TAX	
AGI	**Tax rate**
First $9,000	1.5%
Next $6,000	2.75%
Over $15,000	3.5%

13. Single

0 dependents

AGI = $9,324

_____

14. Married

1 dependent

AGI = $12,618

_____

15. Married

3 dependents

AGI = $37,861

_____

16. Single

0 dependents

AGI = $14,029

_____

17. Married

0 dependents

AGI = $21,355

_____

18. Married

1 dependent

AGI = $38,486

_____

19. Married

3 dependents

AGI = $49,823

_____

20. Single

0 dependents

AGI = $29,342

_____

The Mathematics of Housing and Taxes, SV 9780547625645

Complete the table to find the amount each person owes, or the refund they should get for state and city taxes. Use the tables on page 59.

	Mike, single	Theresa, married, 1 dependent
Adjusted Gross Income	$19,468.12	$32,812.41
State tax withheld	$698.13	$1,214.41
State tax	21. _____	27. _____
State tax owed or refund	22. _____	28. _____
Exemptions (dollar value)	23. _____	29. _____
City taxable income	24. _____	30. _____
City tax withheld	$418.32	$709.21
City tax	25. _____	31. _____
City tax owed or refund	26. _____	32. _____

Problem Solving Strategy: Projecting Estimates

Situation:

Jake is a freelance writer. His paychecks have no taxes withheld from them. He must submit his own estimated tax payments quarterly to the federal, state, and local governments.

Quarterly Estimated Taxes Due:

April 15	June 15	September 15	January 15
_____ →	_____ →	_____ →	_____ →

Strategy:

Projecting estimates can sometimes help you solve a problem.

Applying the Strategy:

A. Last year, Jake paid $4,956 in federal taxes. If Jake expects to earn about the same income this year as last year, how much estimated federal tax should Jake pay on April 15?

THINK: Last year, Jake paid about $5,000 in federal taxes. This year, he expects to earn about the same amount of income. Therefore, he expects to pay about the same in taxes.

Divide by 4 to find the quarterly amount.

$5,000 ÷ 4 = $1,250

Jake should pay $1,250 of estimated federal tax on April 15.

B. Suppose that in August, Jake realized that his income would be greater than he had expected for the year. He estimated that he should pay an additional $1,500 to the federal government, for a total of $6,500. He had already made the April 15 and June 15 payments of $1,250 each. How much will Jake pay on September 15 and January 15?

1. Multiply to find the amount already paid: 2 × $1,250 = $2,500

2. Subtract to find the amount still owed: $6,500 − $2,500 = $4,000

3. Divide by 2 to find the amount of each of the last 2 payments.

$4,000 ÷ 2 = $2,000

Jake will pay $2,000 for each of the last 2 payments.

63

Name _____ Date _____

Practice

Remember to estimate whenever you use your calculator.

Betty estimated that she will need to pay $3,200 in state taxes this year. She divided that amount by 4 and found that she should make four $800 payments during the year. In July, Betty realized that her income would be lower than she had expected. She estimated that she should pay $600 less to the state. She had already made the April 15 and June 15 payments.

1. In July, how much did Betty estimate her state taxes to be?

_____

2. How much money had Betty already paid?

_____

3. How much money did Betty have left to pay?

_____

4. How many payments were left for Betty to make?

_____

5. How much estimated state tax was due on September 15 and on January 15 if both payments were equal?

_____

The Mathematics of Housing and Taxes, SV 9780547625645

Name _____ Date _____

Remember to estimate whenever you use your calculator.

Patrick estimated that he will need to pay $4,600 in state taxes this year. He divided that amount by 4 and found that he should make 4 $1,150 payments during the year. In October, Patrick realized that his income would be higher than expected. He estimated that he should pay an additional $950 to the state. He had already made the April 15, June 15, and September 15 payments.

6. In October, how much did Patrick estimate his state taxes to be? _____

7. How much money had Patrick already paid in state taxes? _____

8. How much money did Patrick have left to pay? _____

9. How many payments were left for Patrick to pay? _____

10. How much estimated tax was due on January 15? _____

This table shows estimated taxes 3 freelance illustrators estimated they should pay this year.

Name	Estimated Taxes		
	Federal	State	City
Victor	$2,800	$960	$240
Ronald	$5,500	$2,000	$550
Mary	$9,000	$3,600	$700

Use the table to solve Exercises 11–16.

11. Victor will make 4 equal estimated tax payments to the state. How much should each payment be?

_____

12. Mary will make 4 equal estimated tax payments to the city. How much should each payment be?

_____

13. Ronald had planned to make 4 equal payments for his federal taxes. After 1 payment, he reduced his estimated federal payment due by $900. How much were each of Ronald's last 3 payments? _____

14. Victor had planned to make 4 equal payments for his federal taxes. After 2 payments, he increased his estimated federal tax due by $1,200. How much were each of Victor's last 2 payments? _____

15. Ronald had planned to make 4 equal payments for his state taxes. After 3 payments, he reduced his estimated state taxes due by $450. How much was Ronald's final payment? _____

16. Mary planned to make 4 equal payments on her federal, state, and city taxes. She now wants to decrease each estimated tax by 15%. How much money will Mary have to spend each quarter to pay all 3 estimated taxes? _____

The Mathematics of Housing and Taxes, SV 9780547625645

This table shows estimated taxes 3 freelance writers estimated they should pay this year.

Name	Estimated Taxes		
	Federal	State	City
Jed	$2,000	$850	$180
Irene	$8,000	$3,000	$600
Burt	$7,000	$2,400	$600

Use the facts in the table to solve the problem.

17. Jed will make 4 equal estimated tax payments to the state. How much should each payment be?

_____

18. Jed will also make 4 equal estimated tax payments to the city. How much should each payment be?

_____

19. Irene had planned to make four $2,000 payments for her federal taxes. After two payments, she reduced her estimated federal tax due by $1,500. How much were each of Irene's last 2 payments?

_____

20. Jed had planned to make four $500 payments for his federal taxes. After one payment, he increased his estimated federal tax due by $900. How much were each of Jed's last 3 payments?

_____

21. Irene had planned to make 4 equal payments for her city taxes. After 2 payments, she lowered her estimated city taxes due by $100. How much were each of Irene's last 2 payments?

_____

22. Burt planned to make 4 equal payments on his federal, state, and city taxes. He now wants to increase each estimated tax by 20%. How much money will Burt have to spend each quarter to pay all 3 estimated taxes?

_____

Decision Making: Choosing the Correct Tax Form

You can use one of three tax forms to file your income taxes: FORM 1040EZ, FORM 1040A, or FORM 1040.

FORM 1040EZ can only be used by single people with no dependents, no adjustments, no itemized deductions, and taxable income less than $100,000.00. Taxable interest cannot exceed $400.00.

FORM 1040A can be used by anyone with taxable income less than $100,000.00. Adjustments are allowable only for Individual Retirement Accounts (IRAs), educator expenses, student loan interest deductions, or tuition and fees deductions. As with form 1040EZ, you cannot itemize deductions.

FORM 1040 can be used by anyone. All adjustments are allowed and deductions can be itemized.

You want to use the simplest form and still pay the lowest allowable tax.

Problem

You are a community tax consultant. Three different people come to you for advice on which tax form to use and how much tax to pay.

	PERSON A	PERSON B	PERSON C
FILING STATUS	SINGLE	MARRIED, JOINT	SINGLE
EXEMPTIONS	1 PERSON, NOT CLAIMED ON ANOTHER RETURN	2 ADULTS	1 PERSON, CLAIMED ON ANOTHER RETURN
WAGES	$25,062	$19,390 AND $27,430	$18,093 AND $7,642 IN TIPS
INTEREST	BANK A: $237 BANK B: $95	BANK: $319 FUND: $116	BANK: $302
ADJUSTMENTS	IRA: $275	IRA: $2,500	NONE
ALLOWABLE DEDUCTIONS			
• MEDICAL	$627	$1079	$295
• TAXES	$935	$618	$308
• INTEREST	$239	$920	$0
• CONTRIBUTIONS	$285	$570	$185
• MISC.	$628	$315	$216

Name _____ Date _____

STANDARD DEDUCTIONS	
Single or married, filing separately	$5,700
Married, filing jointly or qualifying widow(er):	$11,400
Head of household:	$8,400

Decision-Making Comparisons

Complete the table to compare the 3 people. Use the table above for questions 6 and 13.

Factors	Person A	Person B	Person C
Filing Status	Single	7. _____	14. _____
Wages	$25,062	8. _____	15. _____
Interest Income	1. _____	9. _____	$302
Adjustments to income	2. _____	IRA, $2,500	16. _____
Adjusted Gross Income	3. _____	10. _____	$26,037
Exemptions ($3,650 per each allowable exemption)	4. _____	11. _____	$0—no exemptions
Itemized deductions	5. _____	12. _____	$1,004
Standard deduction	6. _____	13. _____	$5,700

17. Which tax form should Person A use? Why?

_____

18. Which tax form should Person B use? Why?

_____

19. Which tax form should Person C use? Why?

_____

Name _____ Date _____

Study the following explanation. Then answer the questions on the following page.

Where To Report Certain Items From 2010 Forms W-2, 1098, and 1099

IRS *e-file* takes the guesswork out of preparing your return. You may also be eligible to use Free File to file your federal income tax return. Visit *www.irs.gov/efile* or see page 38 for details.

Part 1	Items That Can Be Reported on Form 1040EZ	If any federal income tax withheld is shown on the forms in Part 1, include the tax withheld on Form 1040EZ, line 7.
Form	**Item and Box in Which It Should Appear**	**Where To Report on Form 1040EZ**
W-2	Wages, tips, other compensation (box 1) Allocated tips (box 8)	Line 1 See page 10
1099-G	Unemployment compensation (box 1)	Line 3. See page 11
1099-INT	Interest income (box 1) Interest on U.S. savings bonds and Treasury obligations (box 3) Tax-exempt interest (box 8)	Line 2 See the instructions for line 2 beginning on page 10 See the instructions for line 2 beginning on page 10
1099-OID	Original issue discount (box 1) Other periodic interest (box 2)	See the instructions on Form 1099-OID See the instructions on Form 1099-OID
Part 2	**Items That May Require Filing Another Form**	
Form	**Items That May Require Filing Another Form**	**Other Form**
W-2	Advance EIC payment (box 9) Dependent care benefits (box 10) Adoption benefits (box 12, code T) Employer contributions to a health savings account (box 12, code W) Amount reported in box 12, code R or Z	Must file Form 1040A or 1040 Must file Form 1040A or 1040 Must file Form 1040 Must file Form 1040 if required to file Form 8889 (see the instructions for Form 8889) Must file Form 1040
W-2G	Gambling winnings (box 1)	Must file Form 1040
1098-E	Student loan interest (box 1)	Must file Form 1040A or 1040 to deduct
1098-T	Qualified tuition and related expenses (box 1)	Must file Form 1040A or 1040 to claim, but first see the instructions on Form 1098-T
1099-C	Cancelled debt (box 2)	Generally must file Form 1040 (see Pub. 4681)
1099-DIV	Dividends and distributions	Must file Form 1040A or 1040
1099-INT	Interest on U.S. savings bonds and Treasury obligations (box 3) Early withdrawal penalty (box 2) Foreign tax paid (box 6)	See the instructions for line 2 beginning on page 10 Must file Form 1040 to deduct Must file Form 1040 to deduct or take a credit for the tax
1099-LTC	Long-term care and accelerated death benefits	Must file Form 1040 if required to file Form 8853 (see the instructions for Form 8853)
1099-MISC	Miscellaneous income	Must file Form 1040
1099-OID	Early withdrawal penalty (box 3)	Must file Form 1040 to deduct
1099-Q	Qualified education program payments	Must file Form 1040
1099-R	Distributions from pensions, annuities, IRAs, etc.	Must file Form 1040A or 1040
1099-SA	Distributions from HSAs and MSAs*	Must file Form 1040

This includes distributions from Archer and Medicare Advantage MSAs.

Name _____ Date _____

Use the information on pages 67 and 69 to help these people decide which tax form to use.

20. Charlotte Greenaway has unemployment compensation. Can she use Form 1040EZ? Why or why not? What additional forms will she need?

_____

21. David Zucker wants to deduct his student loan interest. Can he file 1040EZ?

_____

22. Jonathan Blondell earned miscellaneous income last year.

_____

23. Katherine Glaston earned $102,321 last year. Can she file 1040A?

_____

24. Steven Rooker earned $19,760 last year, earning a wage in the food service industry. He has no deductions and is single with no dependents. Can he file 1040EZ?

_____

25. Sylvester Renton lives within his means on his pension income. Last year, that income was about $5,000 a month. Can he file 1040EZ?

_____

26. Sandra wants to know which form she needs to file if she won the lottery last year. She has always filed 1040A or 1040EZ in the past.

_____

Money Tips: How Many Deductions Should You Claim?

Let's Look at the Facts

1 or 0 are personal deductions that refer only to you *as an individual*. If you claim 1 deduction, the amount of your weekly paycheck will be greater, since less tax will be taken out. If you claim 0 deductions, your weekly paycheck will be smaller, since more tax will be taken out.

Let's Discuss Why

1. Some people claim 1 deduction because they prefer to get more money in each paycheck. Why might they prefer this?

   _____

   _____

2. If you claim 0 deductions, more tax will be taken out of your paycheck each pay period and you might be entitled to a refund. When would you receive this refund?

   _____

   _____

3. On January 1, you declared 1 deduction on your employment form. On July 1, you changed jobs. You will earn the same salary, but you changed your deduction claim to 0. Next April, at tax time, are you likely to owe money? Get a refund? Neither?

   _____

   _____

4. Many people claim deductions for their spouse, their children, and their home mortgage payments. Tax experts warn that declaring too many deductions may require a large payment plus penalties in April. How can this be avoided?

   _____

   _____

5. Declaring too few deductions may result in a large refund. While this sounds appealing, you could be losing money by doing this. How is this possible?

   _____

   _____

Name _____   Date _____

Let's See What You Would Do

6. You must make car, student loan, and credit card payments every month. Would you prefer to receive more money in your weekly paycheck or receive a large refund later? Explain your decision.

_____

_____

7. By claiming 1 deduction instead of 0, you receive $35 more in each weekly paycheck. What could you do with that extra money that might earn you even more money?

_____

_____

_____

_____

8. You are single and have no debts or financial obligations. Your accountant tells you that you will be getting a $2,300 refund this year. Make a list of all the things you might do with that money.

_____

_____

_____

_____

Calculator: The Memory Keys

You can use calculators with **memory keys** to solve multi-step problems. These are the memory keys.

[M+]	[M−]	[MR] or [RM]	[MC] or [CM]
Adds a number to memory.	Subtracts a number from memory.	Recalls a number from memory.	Clears memory.

Using memory keys, compute: $(15 + 12) + (8 \times 5)$.

Procedure		Calculator Entry	Calculator Display
Step 1	Perform the operation within the first set of parentheses.	[1] [5] [+] [1] [2] [=]	27.
Step 2	Add the result to memory.	[M+]	M 27.
Step 3	Perform the operation within the parentheses.	[8] [×] [5] [=]	M 40.
Step 4	Add the result to memory.	[M+]	M 40.
Step 5	Recall the total in memory.	[MR]	M 67.

So $(15 + 12) + (8 \times 5) = 67$.

Always make sure you clear the memory before you use it.

Name _____ Date _____

Use a calculator to compute.

1. $(5 \times 6) + (3 \times 2) = $ _____

2. $(8 \times 6) - (9 + 2) = $ _____

3. $(11 + 5) + (7 - 3) = $ _____

4. $(14.9 + 6) + (15.6 - 5.2) = $ _____

5. $(9.2 \times 8.3) + (16.2 - 4.5) = $ _____

6. $(248 \times 2.5) - (14.5 + 108) = $ _____

7. $(4.6 \div 2) - (0.4 + 1.3) = $ _____

8. $(0.7 \times 3) + (8 \div 0.2) = $ _____

9. $(0.36 \div 0.3) + (0.8 \div 0.2) = $ _____

Use a calculator to solve.

10. Zelda must pay a 15% tax on her taxable income of $18,000. Her husband must pay a 15% tax on $23,000. How much tax must Zelda and her husband pay?

_____

11. A state income tax is 1% on the first $4,000 and 1.5% on the next $4,000. What would be the total state tax for an income of $7,800?

_____

12. Compare two calculators that have the memory keys in different places. Write a paragraph describing how each performs the functions described on this page and comparing the two machines. Which do you prefer? Why?

_____

_____

_____

_____

Part II Review

Vocabulary

Choose the letter of the word(s) that completes (or complete) the sentence.

1. The W-2 form is used to report _____.

   a. Interest　　　　　　**b.** Wages　　　　　　**c.** Deductions

2. Gross income, less any adjustments, is called _____.

   a. Taxable Income　　**b.** Adjusted Gross Income　　**c.** Unreported Income

3. Amounts that reduce the income to be taxed are called _____.

   a. Deductions　　　　**b.** Exemptions　　　　**c.** Claims

Skills

Find the answer. Use the W-2 and the 1099 forms to find the amount.

4. Wages _____

5. Federal tax withheld _____

6. State tax withheld _____

7. City tax withheld _____

8. Social Security tax withheld _____

9. Interest income _____

10. Gross income _____

22222	a Employee's social security number 000-00-0000	OMB No. 1545-0008		
b Employer identification number (EIN)		1 Wages, tips, other compensation 23,462.18	2 Federal income tax withheld 1,948.72	
c Employer's name, address, and ZIP code		3 Social security wages	4 Social security tax withheld 1,794.86	
Bryant Shoe Co.		5 Medicare wages and tips	6 Medicare tax withheld	
		7 Social security tips	8 Allocated tips	
d Control number		9 Advance EIC payment	10 Dependent care benefits	
e Employee's first name and initial　Last name　Suff.		11 Nonqualified plans	12a	
		13 Statutory employee　Retirement plan　Third-party sick pay	12b	
Calvin Jefferson		14 Other	12c	
			12d	
f Employee's address and ZIP code				
15 State　Employer's state ID number	16 State wages, tips, etc. 23,462,18	17 State income tax 305.18	18 Local wages, tips, etc. 23,462.18	19 Local income tax 183.46　20 Locality name

Form **W-2** Wage and Tax Statement
Copy 1—For State, City, or Local Tax Department

2009

Department of the Treasury—Internal Revenue Service

☐ CORRECTED (if checked)

PAYER'S name, street address, city, state, ZIP code, and telephone no.	Payer's RTN (optional)	OMB No. 1545-0112	
Bryant Credit Union	1 Interest income $ 246.87	**2011**	**Interest Income**
	2 Early withdrawal penalty $	Form **1099-INT**	
PAYER'S federal identification number　RECIPIENT'S identification number	3 Interest on U.S. Savings Bonds and Treas. obligations $		**Copy B For Recipient**
RECIPIENT'S name Calvin Jefferson	4 Federal income tax withheld $	5 Investment expenses $	This is important tax information and is being furnished to the Internal Revenue Service. If you are required to file a return, a
Street address (including apt. no.)	6 Foreign tax paid $	7 Foreign country or U.S. possession	negligence penalty or other sanction may be imposed on you if this income is
City, state, and ZIP code	8 Tax-exempt interest $	9 Specified private activity bond interest $	taxable and the IRS determines that it has not been reported.
Account number (see instructions)	10 Tax-exempt bond CUSIP no. (see instructions)		

Form **1099-INT**　　　(keep for your records)　　Department of the Treasury - Internal Revenue Service

Solve.

11. Sarah's gross income is $27,345. She has $789 in adjustments to income. What is her Adjusted Gross Income?

_____

12. Martin's AGI is $19,456, with a $3,900 deduction and no exemptions. What is his taxable income?

_____

13. Lee Ann's taxable income is $13,932 and she is single. What is her federal tax?

_____

14. Ira files Form 1040EZ and is not claimed on another form. How much is his personal exemption?

_____

15. The Martinez's joint tax return has itemized deductions of $2,780. Should they take the itemized or the standard deduction?

_____

16. Diana's Adjusted Gross Income was $19,874 last year. How much state tax did she pay? (Use the tax table.)

_____

If line 43 (taxable income) is—		And you are—			
At least	But less than	Single	Married filing jointly *	Married filing separately	Head of a house-hold
		Your tax is—			
12,000					
12,000	12,050	1,385	1,203	1,385	1,206
12,050	12,100	1,393	1,208	1,393	1,214
12,100	12,150	1,400	1,213	1,400	1,221
12,150	12,200	1,408	1,218	1,408	1,229
12,200	12,250	1,415	1,223	1,415	1,236
12,250	12,300	1,423	1,228	1,423	1,244
12,300	12,350	1,430	1,233	1,430	1,251
12,350	12,400	1,438	1,238	1,438	1,259
12,400	12,450	1,445	1,243	1,445	1,266
12,450	12,500	1,453	1,248	1,453	1,274
12,500	12,550	1,460	1,253	1,460	1,281
12,550	12,600	1,468	1,258	1,468	1,289
12,600	12,650	1,475	1,263	1,475	1,296
12,650	12,700	1,483	1,268	1,483	1,304
12,700	12,750	1,490	1,273	1,490	1,311
12,750	12,800	1,498	1,278	1,498	1,319
12,800	12,850	1,505	1,283	1,505	1,326
12,850	12,900	1,513	1,288	1,513	1,334
12,900	12,950	1,520	1,293	1,520	1,341
12,950	13,000	1,528	1,298	1,528	1,349
13,000					
13,000	13,050	1,535	1,303	1,535	1,356
13,050	13,100	1,543	1,308	1,543	1,364
13,100	13,150	1,550	1,313	1,550	1,371
13,150	13,200	1,558	1,318	1,558	1,379
13,200	13,250	1,565	1,323	1,565	1,386
13,250	13,300	1,573	1,328	1,573	1,394
13,300	13,350	1,580	1,333	1,580	1,401
13,350	13,400	1,588	1,338	1,588	1,409
13,400	13,450	1,595	1,343	1,595	1,416
13,450	13,500	1,603	1,348	1,603	1,424
13,500	13,550	1,610	1,353	1,610	1,431
13,550	13,600	1,618	1,358	1,618	1,439
13,600	13,650	1,625	1,363	1,625	1,446
13,650	13,700	1,633	1,368	1,633	1,454
13,700	13,750	1,640	1,373	1,640	1,461
13,750	13,800	1,648	1,378	1,648	1,469
13,800	13,850	1,655	1,383	1,655	1,476
13,850	13,900	1,663	1,388	1,663	1,484
13,900	13,950	1,670	1,393	1,670	1,491
13,950	14,000	1,678	1,398	1,678	1,499

STATE TAX	
Adjusted Gross Income	**Tax rate**
First $8,000	2%
Next $7,000	3.5%
Next $5,000	5%
Over $20,000	6.5%

The Mathematics of Housing and Taxes, SV 9780547625645

Part II Test

Ron and Beth are married and filing a joint return. They have 1 child and will take the standard deduction. Use the W-2 forms to find the amount.

1. Total gross income _____

2. Total federal tax withheld _____

3. Total state tax withheld _____

4. Total city tax withheld _____

5. Total Social Security tax withheld

   _____

Find the Adjusted Gross Income, taxable income, and federal tax. Use the federal tax tables on pages 138–144.

6. Single

   Gross income: $47,456

   Adjustments: $569

   Standard deduction: $5,700

   AGI = _____

   Taxable income = _____

   Federal tax = _____

7. Married, filing jointly

   Gross income: $68,709

   Adjustments: $4,231

   Standard deduction: $11,400

   AGI = _____

   Taxable income = _____

   Federal tax = _____

22222	**a** Employee's social security number 000-00-0000	OMB No. 1545-0008		
b Employer identification number (EIN)			**1** Wages, tips, other compensation 17,462.87	**2** Federal income tax withheld 1,215.63
c Employer's name, address, and ZIP code			**3** Social security wages	**4** Social security tax withheld 1,311.46
			5 Medicare wages and tips	**6** Medicare tax withheld
Smith Industries			**7** Social security tips	**8** Allocated tips
d Control number			**9** Advance EIC payment	**10** Dependent care benefits
e Employee's first name and initial Last name Suff.			**11** Nonqualified plans	**12a**
			13 Statutory employee / Retirement plan / Third-party sick pay	**12b**
Ron Showard			**14** Other	**12c**
				12d
f Employee's address and ZIP code				
15 State Employer's state ID number	**16** State wages, tips, etc. 17,462.87	**17** State income tax 219.41	**18** Local wages, tips, etc. 17,462.87	**19** Local income tax 83.16 **20** Locality name

Form **W-2** Wage and Tax Statement   **2009**   Department of the Treasury—Internal Revenue Service
Copy 1—For State, City, or Local Tax Department

22222	**a** Employee's social security number 000-00-0000	OMB No. 1545-0008		
b Employer identification number (EIN)			**1** Wages, tips, other compensation 6,471.32	**2** Federal income tax withheld 416.29
c Employer's name, address, and ZIP code			**3** Social security wages	**4** Social security tax withheld 486.00
			5 Medicare wages and tips	**6** Medicare tax withheld
			7 Social security tips	**8** Allocated tips
d Control number			**9** Advance EIC payment	**10** Dependent care benefits
e Employee's first name and initial Last name Suff.			**11** Nonqualified plans	**12a**
			13 Statutory employee / Retirement plan / Third-party sick pay	**12b**
Beth Showard			**14** Other	**12c**
				12d
f Employee's address and ZIP code				
15 State Employer's state ID number	**16** State wages, tips, etc. 6,471.32	**17** State income tax 119.62	**18** Local wages, tips, etc. 6,471.32	**19** Local income tax 32.11 **20** Locality name

Form **W-2** Wage and Tax Statement   **2009**   Department of the Treasury—Internal Revenue Service
Copy 1—For State, City, or Local Tax Department

Howard's estimated taxes for the year were: Federal: $4,000; State: $1,670; and City: $420.

8. Howard will make 4 equal payments to each, this year. How much should each payment to each

   agency be? _____

9. After 2 payments, Howard lowered his estimated federal taxes due by $300. How much were each of his last 2 federal tax payments?

Part III:
Housing

Pre-Skills Test

Add.

1. $24,850 + $18,920 = _____

2. $57,350 + $9,840 = _____

3. $125,050 + $78,360 = _____

4. $225,100 + $83,692 = _____

Subtract.

5. $93,450 − $71,130 = _____

6. $70,545 − $48,670 = _____

7. $91,800 − $56,072 = _____

8. $130,985 − $87,987 = _____

Multiply.

9. $9 \times $24,000 = _____

10. $4 \times $34,850 = _____

11. $6 \times $108,762 = _____

12. $0.6 \times $123,050 = _____

13. $0.4 \times $90,765 = _____

14. $0.8 \times $86,098 = _____

Find the answer.

15. 6% of $20,000 = _____

16. 9% of $34,500 = _____

17. $5\frac{1}{2}$ % of $58,050 = _____

18. $7\frac{1}{2}$ % of $102,085 = _____

Divide. Round the answer to the nearest cent.

19. $45,000 ÷ 0.3 = _____

20. $38,975 ÷ 0.28 = _____

21. $58,975 ÷ 0.28 = _____

22. $108,764 ÷ 0.28 = _____

Solve the proportion.

23. $\frac{1}{2} = \frac{n}{10}$, $n =$ _____

24. $\frac{2}{5} = \frac{n}{10}$, $n =$ _____

25. $\frac{1}{5} = \frac{n}{20}$, $n =$ _____

26. $\frac{1}{4} = \frac{n}{12}$, $n =$ _____

27. $\frac{1}{1.5} = \frac{n}{12}$, $n =$ _____

28. $\frac{1}{1.5} = \frac{n}{18}$, $n =$ _____

Use the diagram of the room.

29. What is the width? _____

30. What is the length? _____

31. Find the perimeter in feet. _____

32. Find the area in square feet. _____

33. Find the area in square yards. _____

length

12 ft

width
9 ft

Bedroom

Renting an Apartment

Before you look for an apartment, you should know the maximum amount you can afford to spend on **rent**. In general, you should be able to spend a maximum of 28% of your gross monthly pay on rent.

Example 1: Your annual gross salary is $37,440. What is the maximum amount you should be able to spend on rent?

| Step 1 | Divide to find your monthly gross pay. | $37,440 ÷ 12 = $3,120 |

| Step 2 | Multiply to find the maximum rent. |

THINK: 28% = 0.28   0.28 × $3,120 = $873.60

You should be able to spend a maximum of $873.60 a month on rent.

Utilities such as gas and electricity are usually not included in the rent.

Example 2: You want to rent a 1-bedroom apartment in the Moon Lake Apartments. *Plus Utilities* means that you must pay separately for electricity, gas, and water. About how much will you pay each month for both rent and utilities?

THINK: Rent for a one-bedroom apartment = $689. Average monthly electric = $75; average monthly gas = $40; average monthly water = $40

1. Add to find the cost of utilities.
   $75 + $40 + $40 = $155

2. Add to find the total cost.
   $155 + $689 = $844

You will pay about $844 per month for both rent and utilities.

> *Moon Lake Apartments*
>
> $689*   1 bedroom
> $795*   2 bedroom
> $950*   3 bedroom
>
> Plus Utilities
>
> *with one-year lease

You may need to pay a **security deposit** and a **fee** to a rental agent when you move into your apartment. These payments are **move-in costs**.

Example 3: Your rent is $689 per month. You paid 10% of that as a rental fee and two months' rent as a security deposit. What were your move-in costs?

| Step 1 | Multiply to find the rental fee. |

THINK: 10% = 0.1.   0.1 × $689 = $68.90

| Step 2 | Multiply to find the security deposit. | 2 × $689 = $1,378

| Step 3 | Add to find the total move-in costs. | $68.90 + $1,378 = $1,446.90

Your move-in costs were $1,446.90.

Name _____ Date _____

1. What other costs might a person have when moving into his or her first apartment?

_____

_____

_____

2. What other costs might a person have when he or she moves from one apartment to another?

_____

_____

_____

Practice

Remember to estimate whenever you use your calculator.

Find the maximum monthly rent for the gross monthly pay.

1. $2,600 _____

2. $3,750 _____

3. $4,166.67 _____

4. $1,958.96 _____

Find the gross monthly pay and the maximum monthly rent. (Assume that the work week is 40 hours and remember that there are 52 weeks in a year. Round to the nearest cent.)

5. $16,640 per year _____

6. $8.50 per hour _____

7. $9.50 per hour _____

8. $20,800 per year _____

9. $10.50 per hour _____

10. $11 per hour _____

11. $24,960 per year _____

12. $13 per hour _____

13. $14 per hour _____

14. $28,493 per year _____

Use the advertisements for the following problems. Find the total monthly cost for rent, utilities, and extras. Use these amounts for utilities: Electricity = $49 per month; Gas = $37 per month. (No additional charge for water at these apartments.)

The Overlook:
Great price for the location!

Studio: $360
1-bdrm: $385
2-bdrm: $415

– plus utilities –

Eckerson Apartments

1 bdrm. $495*
2 bdrm. $660*
(*plus electricity*)
Health Club—$35/mo extra

Hastings House

1 bdrm. = $375
2 bdrm. = $485
3 bdrm. = $520

(utilities included)

Parking:
$40 per month

---

15. The Overlook, Studio

_____

16. The Overlook, 1 Bedroom

_____

17. Hastings House, 3 Bedrooms + Parking

_____

18. Eckerson Apts., 2 Bedrooms

_____

19. Eckerson Apts., 1 Bedroom

_____

20. The Overlook, 2 Bedrooms

_____

21. Eckerson Apts., 2 Bedrooms + Health Club

_____

22. Who offers the least expensive rent and utilities for 2 Bedrooms?

_____

Name _____ Date _____

Find the move-in costs:

Building:	*The Overlook*	*Hastings House*	*Eckerson Apts.*
Apartment type:	1 bedroom	2 bedrooms	2 bedrooms
Rental agent fee:	75% of 1 month's rent	10% of annual rent	1 month's rent
Security deposit:	2 months' rent	1 month's rent	1.5 months' rent
Total move in costs:	23. _____	24. _____	25. _____

Solve. Remember to estimate whenever you use your calculator.

26. The Wilsons are moving into a $915 apartment they found through a rental agent. The rental fee is 15% of the annual rent. A security deposit of 1.5 months' rent is required. What are the move-in costs? _____

27. The Chens found an apartment that rents for $1,096.75 per month. They do not have to pay a rental fee, but a security deposit of 2 months' rent is required. They paid the first month's rent at the same time they paid move-in costs. How much did they pay in all? _____

28. The Degollados are moving into a $1,000 per month apartment in the Everglen Apartments. They must pay 10% of a month's rent to the rental agent, as well as a 2-month security deposit. How much are their move-in costs? _____

29. Jan Dollinger found a great deal! She can move into a studio apartment at The Scranton for only $450 a month. She'll pay a total of $150 a month for utilities, plus $50 per month more to park her car on the premises. What will she pay each month? _____

30. The Shibargers found a three-bedroom apartment in a good location that's big enough for their growing family. The rent is $1,250 a month, and utilities are additional. Electric runs $70 per month, gas is $50 per month, and water is an additional $45 per month. What will they pay each month? _____

31. Mr. Del Ray's monthly gross income is $4,333.00 a month. How much apartment rent can he afford? _____

The Mathematics of Housing and Taxes, SV 9780547625645

Name _____ Date _____

Problem Solving Application: Renting Apartments

Consumer: Renting Apartments

Statistics show that most young adults live in rental apartments.

When renting an apartment, you need to understand all the costs that are involved. The monthly rent is not your only cost. Usually, you also need to pay a security deposit. The security deposit may be equal to 1 or 2 months' rent.

In some apartment buildings, a charge for gas and electricity is included as part of the rent. In other buildings, you must pay the companies for the gas and electricity used.

Washington Rooming House: Close to Campus; Close to Work

=

More Cost-Effective than Renting an Apartment

Studio................$275/mo
Two rooms...................$355/mo
Three rooms..........................$440/mo
Four rooms.................................$538/mo

Gas and electricity are included.
Security deposit: one month's rent

You decide to rent a single room in Washington Rooming House. How much money will you pay the owner in the first year?

THINK: In the first year, you will need to pay the security deposit plus 12 months' rent.

Step 1   Multiply to find the cost of 12 months' rent. $12 \times \$275 = \$3,300$

Step 2   Add to find the total amount. $\$275 + \$3,300 = \$3,575$
      THINK: The security deposit is equal to 1 month's rent, or $275.

So, you will pay the owner $3,575 in the first year.

     The Mathematics of Housing and Taxes, SV 9780547625645

Here is similar information about Jefferson Manor Rooming House, a competitor. Use the information about the two rooming houses to answer the following exercises. Remember to estimate whenever you use your calculator.

1. What is the monthly rent for a two-room suite in Washington Rooming House? _____

2. What is the monthly rent for a two-room suite in Jefferson Manor Rooming House? _____

3. How much more is the rent for a two-room suite in Jefferson Manor? _____

4. Does the rent for a two-room suite in Jefferson Manor include anything that is not included in the rent for a two-room suite at Washington Rooming House? If so, what?

Jefferson Manor Rooming House:
Clean, Convenient, and Affordable

Studio.................$316/mo
Two rooms....................$404/mo
Three rooms...........................$498/mo
Four rooms.....................................$602/mo

Gas, electricity, and covered parking are included.
Security deposit: one month's rent

---

5. Ann Ramirez has a two-room suite in Washington Rooming House. She bought a car and has to pay to park it nearby. Ann pays $40 a month to park her car. Does she pay more, all things considered, than she would pay to live at Jefferson Manor? _____

6. How much will Ann pay, in rent and parking, in six months (not including security deposit)? _____

Solve.

7. Jack O'Hara rents a two-room suite in Jefferson Manor. He stays for 8 months. How much rent does he pay in the 8 months? _____

8. Danica Diaz rents a three-room suite in Washington Rooming House. She stays one year. Three months into her stay, Danica buys a car. She arranges to park it for $25 a month. At the end of a year, Danica's deposit is returned to her. All things considered, how much has Danica spent during this year, to house herself and park her car? _____

9. In 3 months, Glen Rios pays a total of $1,494 in room rent. Where does he live, and how many rooms is he renting? _____

10. Which is a better deal for someone with a car: two rooms at Washington Rooming House with additional monthly parking of $50.00 a month? Or two rooms at Jefferson Manor? _____

11. John knows he needs three rooms and that he will have no more than $450 per month to spend on housing. He has a bike, but no car. Where can he get the best deal, Washington Rooming House or Jefferson Manor? _____

Name _____   Date _____

Buying a House

You know you will need to borrow money to buy a house. Before you look at houses, you should know the maximum you will be able to borrow and the maximum you will be able to spend for a house. In general, you should borrow no more than 2 times your annual gross income (though some mortgage lenders will tell you otherwise).

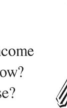

Example 1: You have saved $31,000 to buy a house. Your annual gross income is $48,600. What is the maximum you should be able to borrow? What is the maximum you should be able to spend for a house?

Step 1 Multiply to find the maximum you should borrow. $2 \times \$48,600 = \$97,200$

The maximum you can comfortably borrow is $97,200.

Step 2 Add to find the maximum you can spend. $\$97,200 + \$31,000 = \$128,200$

The maximum you should be able to spend on a house is $128,200.

You would like to buy a house that **appreciates** (increases in value) each year. The more the appreciation, the higher the future value of the house.

Example 2: Fran bought a house for $120,000. Her house appreciated 5% each year. What was the value of the house after 2 years?

Step 1 Multiply to find the first year's appreciation.
THINK: 5% = 0.05

$0.05 \times \$120,000 = \$6,000$

Step 2 Add to find the value after 1 year.

$\$120,000 + \$6,000 = \$126,000$

Step 3 Multiply to find the second year's appreciation.
THINK: Use the value after 1 year.

$\$126,000 \times 0.05 = \$6,300$

Step 4 Add to find the value after 2 years.

$\$126,000 + \$6,300 = \$132,300$

Step 5 Subtract to find the amount of appreciation.

$\$132,300 - \$120,000 = \$12,300$

After two years, Fran's house was worth $12,300 more than she paid for it.

The Mathematics of Housing and Taxes, SV 9780547625645

Practice

TIP Remember to estimate whenever you use your calculator.

These people want to become homeowners. What is the maximum they can afford to borrow? What is the maximum they should be able to spend?

1. Fred Henderson's savings: $18,000
Gross salary: $41,000 per year

_____

2. Denise Chin's savings: $41,600
Gross salary: $36,500 per year

_____

3. Marge LaBeau's savings: $27,620
Gross salary: $785 per week

_____

4. Rafael Rodriguez's savings: $52,600
Gross salary: $71,500 per year

_____

5. Karen Goldblum's savings: $5,000
Gross salary: $3,760 per month

_____

6. The Militanos' savings: $24,409
Gross salaries: Terri $37,200 per year;
Frank $3,975 per month

_____

Complete the table to find the appreciation and the value of each house.

Value	Yearly Rate of Appreciation	Appreciation in One Year	Value After One Year
$50,000	5%	**7.** _____	**8.** _____
$74,500	–3%	–$2,235	**9.** _____
$92,600	1%	**10.** _____	**11.** _____
$140,630	9%	**12.** _____	**13.** _____
$200,000	3%	**14** _____	**15.** _____

Name _____ Date _____

Notice that not all the values in the table above are positive. If a house's value falls in a given year, this is called **depreciation**. The following table shows what happened to one house over a 5-year period. Complete the table.

Year	Value	Yearly Rate of Appreciation	Amount of Appreciation in that Year
Year 1	$250,000	−20%	−$50,000
Year 2	$200,000	16. _____	$0
Year 3	17. _____	4%	$8,000
Year 4	$208,000	18. _____	$4,160
Year 5	19. _____	0%	20. _____

Think About It

1. What factors do you think make a house appreciate or depreciate in value?

_____

_____

_____

More Practice

Solve.

1. Greg's house was valued at $45,500 in 1980. For two years, the house appreciated at a rate of 2% each year. What was the value after 2 years? _____

2. Lillian's house was valued at $170,500 in 2003. The house appreciated 6.5% each year. What was the value after 2 years? _____

3. Fawn's house in Connecticut was valued at $155,000 in 1981. The house appreciated 10% each year for the first 2 years. What was the value after 2 years? _____

4. Michelle's house was valued at $166,400. The house appreciated 9.5% each year. What was the value after 2 years? _____

5. Gene's house was valued at $248,200 when he bought it. The house appreciated at 12.5% per year for the next three years. What was the value after 3 years? (Round your answer to the nearest cent.)

_____

6. Hal and Donna's house in Anchorage was valued at $103,600 in 1988. The house depreciated at a rate of 2% per year (**THINK:** reduced in value by 2% per year), for the next 2 years. What was the house worth in 1990? _____

7. John and Sharon bought a house in Seattle in 2007 for $465,000. In 2008, it depreciated 10%. How much was the house then worth? _____

8. Janet bought a house for $358,000. The following year, it was worth only $304,300. At what rate did it depreciate that year? _____

9. Gary's house was valued at $582,500. For the next two years, it depreciated at a rate of 5% each year. What was it worth after 2 years? _____

10. Shauna's house was worth $140,000 when she bought it. It held its value for one year (i.e., neither appreciated nor depreciated), but the following year it lost 2% of its value. What was it worth after 2 years? _____

Extension   **Appreciation**

Just because a house costs more than another does not mean that it will be more valuable in the future. Ed bought a house for $53,900. It appreciated 13% each year. Eileen bought a house for $61,000. It appreciated 6% each year.

1. Which house was worth more after 2 years?

_____

2. If the houses keep appreciating in the same way, what will the difference in value be in 5 years? _____

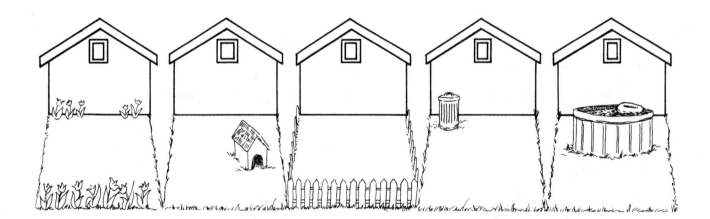

Buying a Condominium

A **condominium** is a building in which apartments are owned. You purchase an apartment just as you would purchase a house. As the owner of an individual condo, or apartment, you pay an additional monthly **maintenance fee** (also called **condominium dues**, or **Homeowners' Association (HOA) dues**) for the care of the building and the grounds. The maintenance fee may include utilities.

Village Park Condominiums
Unit 801

2 beds | 2.5 bath | 1894 Sq. Ft.   For Sale: $167,000

| Pictures | Virtual Tours |

Unit Information:

MLS # 0000000000   Association Fees: $250/m
Taxes: $4,900/y   County: Tompkin
Views: Hill Country   Year Built: 2005

Unit Amenities:

General:	**Appliances:**	**Garage:**
2-story	Disposal	2-car
Utility Room	Microwave	attached
1 Fireplace	Dishwasher	**Roof:** Composition shingle
Region: Longacre	Central A.C.	

Example 1: As your first home, you bought the small condo shown in the advertisement on page 91. How much did you put down? How much will you pay each month?

(**THINK:** Price = $167,000; Down payment = 20%, or 0.2; Loan payment = $800.99 per month; maintenance fee = $250 per month)

Step 1 Find the down payment. $0.2 \times \$167,000 = \$33,400$

You put down $33,400.

Step 2 Add to find the total monthly payment. $\$800.99 + \$250 = \$1,050.99$

You will pay $1,050.99 per month.

Remember that you should be able to spend 28% of your gross monthly pay for housing. When buying a condominium, that 28% includes maintenance, mortgage payment, taxes, and insurance.

You can roughly estimate the gross monthly pay you will need to afford the condominium by just using the loan payment and the maintenance fee.

Example 2: The monthly payments for the condominium in Example 1 are $1,050.99. Roughly estimate the least you could earn each month to afford the condominium.

(**THINK:** $1,050.99 is about $1,100; 0.28 is about 0.3.)

If monthly housing cost	=	$0.3 \times$ gross monthly pay,
Then gross monthly pay	=	monthly housing cost $\div$ 0.3
	=	$3,666.67

To afford the condominium, your gross monthly pay would need to be at least $3,666.67. In fact, it would need to be more in order to cover the additional cost of taxes and homeowner's insurance.

Name _____ Date _____

1. Why might someone choose to buy a condominium instead of a house?

   _____

   _____

   _____

2. Condominium maintenance fees are not fixed; they go up as expenses go up. What problems could this cause for the homeowner?

   _____

   _____

   _____

Practice

Remember to estimate whenever you use your calculator.

Find the downpayment and the total monthly payment for the condominium (mortgage plus maintenance fees):

Fox Run Condominiums $178,000; HOA dues $400/ mo; 20% down; $853.76/mo	Cliffside Condos $250,000; HOA dues $550/mo; 20% down; $1,073.64/mo	Tintara Condominiums $100,000; HOA dues $220/ mo; 3.5% down; $578.56/mo
1. _____	2. _____	3. _____

Calculate the minimum gross monthly pay needed to afford the following condominium total loan and maintenance payments.

4. $980 _____

5. $1,250 _____

6. $2,200 _____

7. $2,780 _____

8. $3,550 _____

9. $4,000 _____

Solve.

10. Pete bought a condominium for $187,600. He put 20% down and pays $899.80 per month. The maintenance fee is $350 per month. Find the down payment and the total monthly payment.

_____

11. Lorraine's condo cost $175,000. She put 20% down and pays $751.55 per month. The monthly maintenance fee is $278. Find the down payment and the total monthly payment. _____

12. Colleen wants to buy a condominium with monthly payments of $1,010. Roughly estimate the minimum gross monthly pay she needs to afford it. _____

Extension	**Planning Ahead for Maintenance Fees**

Brian wants to buy the condominium described in the advertisement. He thinks that the maintenance fee will go up 40% over the next 2 years.

1. If Bryan is right, what will the maintenance fee be in 2 years?

_____

2. Assuming his mortgage rate is fixed, what will his monthly payment be in 2 years?

_____

Cloverleaf Condos: $287,450

Financing with 20% down: $1,234.47/mo.

Maintenance: $150/mo

Getting a Mortgage

The loan you get to buy a house or a condominium is called a **mortgage**. The **principal and interest ("P&I")** portion of your monthly mortgage payment depends on the amount you borrow, the **interest rate**, and the total number of payments (the mortgage **term**).

Mortgage rates go up or down as a result of a variety of economic factors. In 1985, some 30-year mortgages had an interest rate of almost 12%. In 2010, the rate was closer to 5%, or even less. Rates vary a bit by region, and housing prices differ, as well.

Example 1: Your parents bought a house when they were first married. It cost $82,750. They put 20% down and borrowed the remainder at 10.5% for 30 years. What was the **down payment** and the mortgage amount? How much did they pay each month?

Step 1 Multiply to find the down payment.

(**THINK:** 20% = 0.2)

$0.2 \times \$82,750 = \$16,550$

The down payment was $16,550.

Step 2 Subtract to find the mortgage amount.

$\$82,750 - \$16,550 = \$66,200$

The mortgage amount was $66,200.

Step 3 Divide to find how many $1,000 you are borrowing.

$\$66,200 \div \$1,000 = 66.2$

Step 4 Multiply to find the monthly payment.

(**THINK:** Use the mortgage payment table. Find the monthly payment per $1,000, or $9.15.)

$66.2 \times \$9.15 = \$605.73$

They paid $605.73 per month.

MORTGAGE PAYMENTS PER $1000			
Interest Rate	Monthly Payment		
	20-y loan	25-y loan	30-y loan
5.0%	$6.60	$5.85	$5.37
5.5%	$6.88	$6.14	$5.68
6.0%	$7.16	$6.44	$6.00
6.5%	$7.46	$6.75	$6.32
7.0%	$7.75	$7.07	$6.65
7.5%	$8.06	$7.39	$6.99
8.0%	$8.36	$7.72	$7.34
8.5%	$8.68	$8.05	$7.69
9.0%	$9.00	$8.40	$8.05
9.5%	$9.33	$8.74	$8.41
10.0%	$9.66	$9.09	$8.78
10.5%	$9.99	$9.45	$9.15
11.0%	$10.33	$9.81	$9.53
11.5%	$10.66	$10.16	$9.90
12.0%	$11.01	$10.53	$10.29
12.5%	$11.36	$10.90	$10.67
13.0%	$11.72	$11.28	$11.06
13.5%	$12.07	$11.66	$11.45
14.0%	$12.44	$12.04	$11.85
14.5%	$12.80	$12.42	$12.25
15.0%	$13.17	$12.81	$12.64
15.5%	$13.54	$13.20	$13.05

Name _____ Date _____

The **closing** is the day on which you sign the mortgage papers and the contract. You will have to pay **closing costs** to the bank and others who helped process the mortgage. Included in these costs are whatever **points** you have agreed to pay. You can sometimes reduce your interest rate by paying points "up front," which means at closing. Each point is 1% of the mortgage amount.

Example 2: Your parents' mortgage amount was $66,200. Their closing costs were $2\frac{1}{2}$ points, plus $250 for the bank's attorney, and a $185 title fee. How much were their closing costs?

(**THINK:** $2\frac{1}{2}$ points $= 2\frac{1}{2}\% = 0.025$)

| Step 1 | Multiply to find the points. | $0.025\% \times \$66,200 = \$1,655$ |

| Step 2 | Add to find the closing costs. | $\$1,655 + \$250 + \$185 = \$2,090$ |

Their closing costs were $2,090.

Think About It

1. How could you estimate the extra cost per month of borrowing $50,000 for 30 years at 11% instead of 10%?

_____

_____

_____

Practice

Using the table, find the monthly payment on the following mortgages to the nearest cent.

Mortgage amount	Interest Rate	Term	Monthly payment
$145,000	10.5%	30 y	**1.** _____
$98,000	11.5%	25 y	**2.** _____
$220,000	6%	20 y	**3.** _____
$175,000	5%	30 y	**4.** _____
$114,000	8.5%	30 y	**5.** _____

The Mathematics of Housing and Taxes, SV 9780547625645

Name _____ Date _____

For the following mortgages, calculate the down payment amount, the mortgage amount, and the monthly payment:

Purchase Price	% Down	Down payment	Mortgage amt.	Interest rate	Term	Monthly payment
$124,000	20%	6. _____	7. _____	10.5%	30 y	8. _____
$89,700	10%	9. _____	10. _____	10.0%	20 y	11. _____
$93,620	30%	12. _____	13. _____	11.0%	25 y	14. _____
$79,840	15%	15. _____	16. _____	9.5%	30 y	17. _____

Find the closing costs.

Mortgage amount	Points	Attorney's Fees	Title Fees	Closing Costs
$37,000	3	$750	$300	18. _____
$57,000	1	$900	$250	19. _____
$109,500	4	$840	$175	20. _____
$96,450	2½	$575	$375	21. _____
$88,750	3½	$465	$305	22. _____

When housing costs go up and rates go down, the numbers look a little different.

Calculate down payment, mortgage amount, and monthly payment for these higher purchase prices with lower interest rates:

Purchase Price	% Down	Down payment	Mortgage amt.	Rate	Term	Monthly payment
$189,000	20%	23. _____	24. _____	5.5%	30 y	25. _____
$289,700	10%	26. _____	27. _____	5.0%	20 y	28. _____
$393,000	30%	29. _____	30. _____	6.0%	25 y	31. _____
$479,000	25%	32. _____	33. _____	6.5%	30 y	34. _____

Extension | **Using Bank Websites**

Most banks post their rates at their websites. Their rates vary, not in increments of 0.5%, as in the table on page 95, but in increments of 0.125% (an eighth). Use the table to answer the questions that follow. The example uses a 30-year fixed-rate mortgage.

Using the table, find the monthly payment on the following mortgages to the nearest cent.

Assume the term of the mortgage is 30 years.

1. $145,000 at 5% _____

2. $98,000 at 6.875% _____

3. $220,000 at 5.625% _____

4. $175,000 at 5.375% _____

5. $114,000 at 6.125% _____

6. $151,200 at 5.25% _____

7. $260,750 at 6.375% _____

8. $275,100 at 7% _____

9. $359,250 at 5.5% _____

10. $100,000 at 5.875% _____

MORTGAGE PAYMENTS PER $1000	
Interest Rate	Monthly Payment
	30-y loan
5.0%	$5.37
5.125%	$5.44
5.25%	$5.52
5.375%	$5.60
5.5%	$5.68
5.625%	$5.76
5.75%	$5.84
5.875%	$5.92
6.0%	$6.00
6.125%	$6.08
6.25%	$6.16
6.375%	$6.24
6.5%	$6.32
6.625%	$6.40
6.75%	$6.49
6.875%	$6.57
7.0%	$6.65

98

Real Estate Taxes

Local governments collect **real estate taxes**. The taxes are used to pay for municipal services and schools. The real estate tax is based on the assessed valuation of a property. The **assessed valuation** is a percent of the property's **market value**. The tax rate is an amount per $100 of assessed valuation.

Example 1: The market value of your property is $88,700. The assessment rate is 70%. What is the assessed valuation? If the real estate tax rate is $4.29 per $100, what is your annual real estate tax?

$$\text{Assessed Valuation} = \text{Assessment Rate} \times \text{Market Value}$$

Step 1 Multiply to find the assessed valuation.
(**THINK:** 70% = 0.7)

$0.7 \times \$88,700 = \$62,090$

The assessed valuation of your property is $62,090.

Step 2 Divide to find the number of $100 of assessed valuation.
$\$62,090 \div \$100 = 620.9$

Step 3 Multiply to find the real estate tax.
$620.9 \times \$4.29 = \$2,663.661$

Your annual real estate tax is $2,663.66.

Many people pay $\frac{1}{12}$ of their annual real estate tax with their monthly mortgage payment. The bank then pays the taxes when they are due.

Example 2: Your monthly mortgage payment is $487. Your annual real estate tax is $2,663.66. Assuming you have agreed to have the bank include a portion of your taxes as part of your monthly mortgage payment, what is your combined "P.I.T." (principal, interest, and taxes) monthly payment to the bank?

Step 1 Divide to find the monthly tax payment.
$\$2,663.66 \div 12 = \$221.97166 \approx \$221.97$

Step 2 Add to find the combined "P.I.T." payment.
$\$221.97 + \$487 = \$708.97$

Your combined PIT payment is $708.97.

Name _____ Date _____

1. Why might the tax rate in a town increase?

_____

_____

2. How could a bank earn money for itself by collecting $\frac{1}{12}$ of the real estate taxes each month and holding the money until the tax payment is due?

_____

_____

Practice

Remember to estimate whenever you use your calculator.

Find the assessed valuation.

Market Value	$95,000	$118,000	$172,900	$287,300	$398,450
Assessment rate	80%	75%	100%	45%	78%
Assessed valuation	**1.** _____	**2.** _____	**3.** _____	**4.** _____	**5.** _____

Find the annual real estate tax.

Assessed valuation	$64,300	$51,700	$39,200	$80,400	$107,650
Tax rate per $100	$3.72	$4.06	$5.04	$2.89	$4.87
Annual real estate tax	**6.** _____	**7.** _____	**8.** _____	**9.** _____	**10.** _____

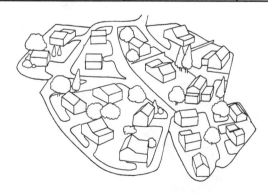

Name _____   Date _____

Find the combined monthly payment to the bank.

Monthly mortgage payment	$413	$397	$516	$471	$507
Annual real estate tax	$3,696	$5,124	$4,344	$3,708	$5,256
Combined monthly payment	11. _____	12. _____	13. _____	14. _____	15. _____

Solve.

16. The market value of Sara's house is $125,000. The assessment rate is 70%. What is the assessed valuation? _____

17. The market value of Tony's house is $95,000. The assessment rate is 55%. What is the assessed valuation? _____

18. The market value of Rudy's house is $135,000. The assessment rate is 65%. The real estate tax rate is $3.29 per $100. What is the assessed valuation and his annual real estate tax? _____

19. The market value of Kathy's house is $89,900. The assessment rate is 80%. The real estate.tax rate is $4.23 per $100. What is the assessed valuation and her annual real estate tax? _____

20. Rudy's monthly mortgage payment is $564. Use your answer to Exercise 18 to find his combined monthly payment to the bank. _____

21. Kathy's monthly mortgage payment is $459. Use your answer to Exercise 19 to find her combined monthly payment to the bank. _____

Name _____ Date _____

Solve the following problem.

1. The average house in a town has a market value of $100,000. The assessment rate is 80% ($80,000 assessed valuation) and the tax rate is $4.00 per $100 ($3,200 annual taxes). The town is going to change to an assessment rate of 100% (or, roughly, market value), but they still want to collect roughly $3,200 annually from the average house. What should the new tax rate be, per $100 of value? How did you solve the problem?

_____

_____

_____

Name _____   Date _____

Homeowner's Insurance

If you own a house or condominium or rent an apartment, you need **homeowner's insurance**. Homeowner's insurance pays for damage to your property and belongings and provides liability coverage in case someone is injured on your property.

You should insure a home or condominium for its full **replacement value**, or the amount it would cost to reconstruct it if destroyed. If you insure for 100% replacement value, then your insurance company will provide these additional coverages.

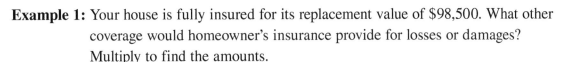

Mutual Insurance Company
1111 Main Street
Marshall, MO 22222

Valued Customer:

Other structure (garage, etc.):   10% of house-replacement value

Personal property: 50% of house-replacement value

Additional living expenses while
   house is being repaired or replaced: 20% of house-replacement value

Trees, shrubs, plants: 5% of house-replacement value

Example 1: Your house is fully insured for its replacement value of $98,500. What other coverage would homeowner's insurance provide for losses or damages?

Multiply to find the amounts.

Other structures (10%)	$0.1 \times \$98,500 = \$9,850$
Personal property (50%)	$0.5 \times \$98,500 = \$49,250$
Living expenses (20%)	$0.2 \times \$98,500 = \$19,700$
Trees, shrubs, plants (5%)	$0.05 \times \$98,500 = \$4,925$

The Mathematics of Housing and Taxes, SV 9780547625645

Name _____ Date _____

If you rent, you should get homeowner's insurance to cover the full replacement value of your personal property against losses due to fire or theft. Then the insurance company will provide these additional coverages.

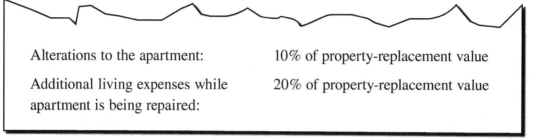

Alterations to the apartment:	10% of property-replacement value
Additional living expenses while apartment is being repaired:	20% of property-replacement value

Example 2: Gail rents and fully insures her personal property for $129,250. What other coverage would homeowner's insurance provide for losses or damage?

Multiply to find the amounts.

Alterations (10%) $0.1 \times \$129{,}250 = \$12{,}925$

Living expenses (20%) $0.2 \times \$129{,}250 = \$25{,}850$

Think About It

1. Statistics show that 96% of homeowners, but only 32% of renters, have insurance. Why is that?

_____

_____

_____

2. What are the dangers of not having homeowner's insurance?

_____

_____

_____

Name _____ Date _____

Practice

Remember to estimate whenever you use your calculator.

Complete the table to show the coverages provided for the homeowner. The home is insured for its full replacement value.

Home-replacement value	Other structures	Personal property	Additional living expenses	Trees, shrubs, plants
$78,000	1. _____	2. _____	3. _____	4. _____
$109,500	5. _____	6. _____	7. _____	8. _____
$87,645	9. _____	10. _____	11. _____	12. _____

Complete the table to show the coverages provided for the renter. Personal property is insured for its full replacement value.

Personal property-replacement value	Alterations to apartment	Additional living expenses
$25,000	13. _____	14. _____
$50,000	15. _____	16. _____
$75,000	17. _____	18. _____

Extension **Fire Prevention**

Cause of Fire in Homes

The circle graph shows the leading causes of fires in the United States. There were about 868,000 fires in 1 year. About how many of them were caused by:

1. heating equipment? _____

2. cooking? _____

3. children playing? _____

4. smoking? _____

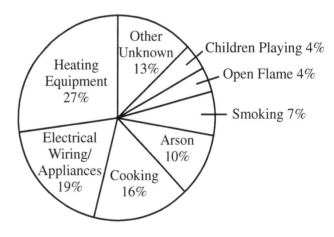

5. Based on these statistics, what steps could you take to reduce fire hazards in your home?

_____

_____

The Mathematics of Housing and Taxes, SV 9780547625645

Name _____ Date _____

Think again about what other coverage homeowner's insurance provides for losses or damages.

(**THINK:** Multiply to find the amount of each additional coverage.)

- Other structures: insured up to 10% of replacement value
- Personal property: insured up to 50% of replacement value
- Additional living expenses: insured up to 20% of replacement value
- Trees, shrubs, plants: insured up to 5% of replacement value

Complete the table. Use the information above to find the coverages provided for each of the 5 homeowners. Assume that the home is insured for its full replacement value.

Home-replacement value	Other structures	Personal property	Additional living expenses	Trees, etc.
$122,000	6. _____	7. _____	8. _____	9. _____
$192,800	10. _____	11. _____	12. _____	13. _____
$107,200	14. _____	15. _____	16. _____	17. _____
$82,850	18. _____	19. _____	20. _____	21. _____
$261,240	22. _____	23. _____	24. _____	25. _____

The Mathematics of Housing and Taxes, SV 9780547625645

Utilities

The cost of **utilities** such as electricity, water, natural gas, or heating oil are part of your living costs. **Meters** keep track of how much electricity, water, and natural gas are used. An electric meter shows the number of **kilowatt-hours** (kWh).

1 kWh is 1,000 watts of electricity used for 1 hour.

Example 1: Read the electric meter. When the pointer is between 2 numbers, read the lower number.

The meter reads 56,901 kWh.

You pay for electricity by the kWh.

Example 2: On April 1, your electric meter read 54,095 kWh. On May 1, the meter read 56,901 kWh. A kWh costs $0.0528. How much did it cost you for the electricity used from April 1 to May 1?

Cost of Electricity = Cost Per kWh × kWh

Step 1 Subtract to find the number of kWh used.
56,901 − 54,095 = 2,806

Step 2 First estimate the cost.
3,000 × $0.05 = $150

Step 3 Then multiply to find the exact cost.
2,806 × $0.0528 = $148.1568

The electricity cost $148.16. The answer is reasonable since it is close to the estimate, which is $150.

You usually pay for the natural gas you use in units of 100 cubic feet.

Example 3: During April, you used 184 hundred cubic feet of gas. Gas costs $0.6133 per 100 cubic feet. How much did it cost you for gas during April?

| Step 1 | First estimate the cost.
200 × $0.60 = $120

| Step 2 | Then multiply to find the exact cost.
184 × $0.06133 = $112.8472

The gas cost $112.85. The answer is reasonable since it is close to the estimate, $120.

You usually pay for the water you use in units of 1,000 cubic feet.

Example 4: From July through August, you used 2,890 cubic feet of water. Water costs $14.38 per 1,000 cubic feet. How much did it cost you for water?

| Step 1 | Divide to find the number of 1,000 cubic ft.
2,890 ÷ 1,000 = 2.89.

| Step 2 | First estimate the cost.
3 × $14 = $42

| Step 3 | Then multiply to find the exact cost.
2.89 × $14.38 = $41.5582

The water cost $41.56. The answer is reasonable since it is close to the estimate, $42.

Think About It

1. How could you estimate the savings that would result from using less electricity?

_____

_____

2. Is more electricity used in summer or in winter? Why?

_____

_____

Practice

Remember to estimate whenever you use your calculator.

Read the electric meter.

1. _____

2. _____

3. _____

Complete the table to find the kWh used and the cost of the electricity.

Second reading	First reading	kWh used	Cost per kWh	Total cost
52,038 kWh	49,165 kWh	**4.** _____	$0.0493	**5.** _____
9,607 kWh	8,406 kWh	**6.** _____	$0.0603	**7.** _____
60,831 kWh	43,194 kWh	**8.** _____	$0.0238	**9.** _____
19,743 kWh	12,162 kWh	**10.** _____	$0.0537	**11.** _____

Find the cost of gas.

100 cubic ft used	141	159	933	222
Cost per 100 cubic ft	$0.5879	$0.9482	$0.0328	$0.6934
Cost of gas	**12.** _____	**13.** _____	**14.** _____	**15.** _____

109

Name _____ Date _____

Complete the table to find the number of 1,000 cubic ft and the cost of water.

Cubic ft used	1,000 cubic ft used	Cost per 1,000 cubic ft	Total cost
3,051	16. _____	$14.38	17. _____
2,134	18. _____	$13.50	19. _____
4,892	20. _____	$11.23	21. _____
4,809	22. _____	$15.85	23. _____

| **Extension** | **Monthly Costs of Owning a Home** |

**This circle graph shows the percents of monthly payments
the average homeowner spends on mortgage, taxes, utilities,
and insurance. A homeowner spends about $1,450 per
month on expenses. About how much is spent on:**

1. Mortgage? _____

2. Utilities? _____

3. Taxes? _____

4. Insurance? _____

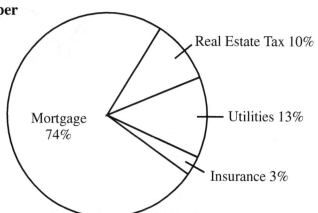

Mortgage 74%
Real Estate Tax 10%
Utilities 13%
Insurance 3%

The Mathematics of Housing and Taxes, SV 9780547625645

Problem Solving Application: Cost of Electricity

The amount of electrical power used by appliances varies. The table below shows the approximate power used in an hour by electrical appliances. If the cost of electricity per kilowatt-hour is known, as well as the number of hours an appliance is used, the electrical costs can be computed.

Appliance	Power used (kW)
Air conditioner	1.250
Clothes dryer	3.750
Radio	0.125
Refrigerator	0.250
Television	0.225
Toaster	0.775
Vacuum cleaner	0.550

The television set is used an average of 4 hours per day. If the cost of electricity is $0.14 per kilowatt-hour, what is the cost of electricity for the television set for a year (365 days)?

1. Multiply to find the number of hours the television is used per year.

Hours used per day	×	Number of days	=	Hours used per year
4	×	365	=	1,460

2. Multiply to find the cost of using the set for 1 hour

Power in kilowatts	×	Cost per kilowatt-hour	=	Cost of use per hour
0.225	×	$0.14	=	$0.0315

3. Multiply the number of hours by the cost per hour.
1,460 × $0.0315 = $45.99

So, the cost of electricity for the television is $45.99 per year.

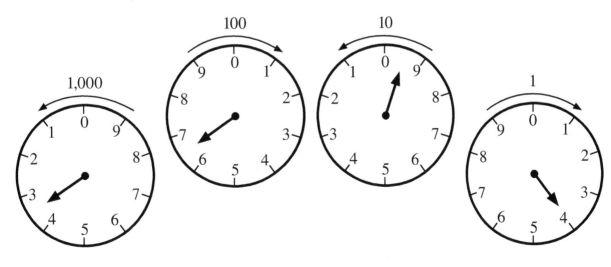

Name _____ Date _____

Use the table to find the cost. Assume the cost of electricity is $0.14 per kilowatt-hour. One year is 365 days, or 52 weeks.

1. The air conditioner is used 8 hours per day for 60 days. _____

2. The vacuum cleaner is used an average of 2 hours per week for 1 year. _____

3. The refrigerator is used 24 hours per day for a year. _____

4. The radio is used 6 hours per day for 1 year. _____

Use $0.16 as the cost of electricity per kilowatt-hour in problems 5–8.

5. The clothes dryer is used an average of 4 hours per week for 1 year. _____

6. The air conditioner is used 9 hours per day for 60 days. _____

7. The toaster is used 10 minutes a day for 60 days. _____

8. Which appliance costs about $0.60 an hour to use? _____

Problem Solving Application: Energy Conservation

The Johnson family owns a 3-bedroom home that is heated by oil. Their furnace uses an average of 90 gallons per month. A consumer magazine provides a report about a new thermostat that can cut the use of home heating oil by 15%. The Johnsons are interested in purchasing this new thermostat.

How many gallons of oil will be saved using this new thermostat for 4 months?

Step 1 Write an equation. Use the formula $s = 0.15 \times 90 \times t$.
Let s represent the amount of oil saved and t the amount of time.
(**THINK:** Amount of oil saved is 4 times 15% of 90 gal)

(**WRITE:**	s	$=$	$4\,(0.15 \times 90)$

Step 2 Solve.

	s	$=$	$4\,(13.5)$
	s	$=$	54

So, using the new thermostat for 4 months will save 54 gallons of oil.

Name _____ Date _____

1. The Johnson family uses an *average* of 90 gallons of oil per month. What does this statement mean?

_____

_____

2. During what time of year will the Johnson family see the most savings?

_____

_____

Solve. Use the formula $s = 0.15 \times 90 \times t$.

1. How many gallons of oil would be saved in 36 months? _____

2. About how many months would it take to save 400 gal of oil? _____

3. About how many months would it take to save 650 gal of oil? _____

4. How many gallons of oil would be saved in $4\frac{1}{2}$ years? _____

Suppose oil costs \$1.10 per gallon. Solve.

5. How much less money would you pay for oil in 12 months with the new thermostat? _____

6. How much money would be saved in 3.5 years with the new thermostat? _____

Name _____ Date _____

Decorating and Remodeling

You decide to paint the living room walls. You want to make only 1 trip to the paint store to get the paint, so you use the accepted guideline: 1 gallon of paint covers about 400 square feet (including spaces for windows and doors).

Example 1: The ceiling in the room is 8 feet high. How many gallons of paint will you need to paint the walls? How much will the paint cost at $16.85 per gallon (including tax)?

(**THINK:** Identify the dimensions of the room.)

Length = 18 ft   Width = 14 ft   Height = 8 ft

Step 1 Add to find the perimeter.
14 + 18 + 14 + 18 = 64 ft

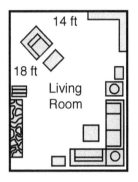

Step 2 Multiply to find the area of the 4 walls.
8 × 64 = 512 square ft

Step 3 Divide to find the number of gallons.
512 ÷ 400 = 1.28 gal

Since 1.28 gal > 1 gal, you will need 2 gallons of paint.

Step 4 Multiply to find the cost.
2 × $16.85 = $33.70

The paint will cost $33.70.

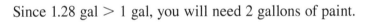

Denise hired a contractor to remodel her living room and porch.
Remodeling means entirely rebuilding 1 or more rooms.
Contractors often quote remodeling costs by the square foot.

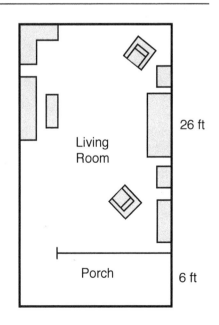

Example 2: The contractor charged $18 per square foot to remodel the living room and $8 per square foot to remodel the porch. How much did the remodeling cost?

(**THINK:** Identify the dimensions of the rooms.)

Living room: 26 ft by 18 ft   Porch: 18 ft by 6 ft

Step 1 Multiply to find the area of each room.
Living room: $26 \times 18 = 468$ sq. ft
Porch: $18 \times 6 = 108$ sq. ft

Step 2 Multiply to find the cost of remodeling each room.
Living room: $468 \times \$18 = \$8,424$
Porch: $108 \times \$8 = \$864$

Step 3 Add to find the total cost.
$\$8,424 + \$864 = \$9,288$

It cost $9,288 to remodel the living room and the porch.

Scale drawings help people decide where to place furniture in a room. You can use a proportion to find scale dimensions.

Example 3: A room is 12 feet long by 9 feet wide. You use a scale of 1 in. = 1.5 ft. What is the scale width of the room?

Step 1 Write a proportion. $\dfrac{1}{1.5} = \dfrac{w}{9}$ ⟵ scale / ⟵ actual

Step 2 Cross multiply. $\dfrac{1}{1.5} \times \dfrac{w}{9}$

Step 3 Solve for w. $1.5w = 9$
$w = 9 \div 1.5$
$w = 6$

The scale width is 6 in.

Name _____ Date _____

1. For rooms with 8-foot ceilings, why could you buy 1 gallon of paint for every 50 feet of perimeter?

_____

_____

2. How could you use a scale drawing to decide where to put furniture?

_____

_____

Practice

Remember to estimate whenever you use your calculator.
Find the perimeter of the room.

1. 14 ft by 15 ft _____

2. 9 ft by 12 ft _____

3. 13 ft by 15 ft _____

4. 12 ft by 18 ft _____

How many gallons of paint are needed to paint the walls? How much will the paint cost?

5. Room: 14 ft by 15 ft
   Ceiling: 8 ft
   Paint: $13.95/gal

   _____

6. Room: 16 ft by 20 ft
   Ceiling: 8 ft
   Paint: $17.05/gal

   _____

7. Room: 24 ft by 38 ft
   Ceiling: 8 ft
   Paint: $10.65/gal

   _____

How much will the remodeling cost?

8. Room: 9 ft by 12 ft
   Cost: $14/square ft

   _____

9. Room: 14 ft by 16 ft
   Cost: $9/square ft

   _____

10. Basement: 12 ft by 24 ft
    Cost: $10.50/square ft

    _____

Find the scale dimensions of the room.

11. Room: 12 ft by 15 ft
Scale: 1 in = 1.5 ft

_____

12. Room: 15 ft by 20 ft
Scale: 2 in = 5 ft

_____

13. Room: 12 ft by 15 ft
Scale: 5 cm = 2 ft

_____

```
┌─────────────┬──────────────┬─────────────┐
│   20 ft     │    14 ft     │    11 ft     │
│             │              │              │
│             │ Living Room  │ Breakfast Nook│
│             │              │              │
│             ├──────────────┴─────────────┤
│ 24 ft  Family Room                        │
│             ┌──────────────┬─────────────┤
│             │              │              │
│             │ Dining Room  │ 12 ft  Kitchen│
│             │              │              │
│             │    12 ft     │    13 ft     │
└─────────────┴──────────────┴─────────────┘
```

FIRST FLOOR All ceilings are 8 ft high.

Use the scale drawing for Exercises 14–19.

14. How many gallons of paint should be bought to paint the living room walls? How much would the paint cost at $17.85 per gallon? _____

15. How many gallons of paint should be bought to paint the walls of all of the rooms? How much would the paint cost at $16.35 per gallon? _____

16. How much would it cost to remodel the dining room at $11.50 per square foot? _____

17. How much would it cost to remodel the entire first floor at $9.20 per square foot? _____

18. What would be the scale dimensions of the family room if the scale were 1 in. = 1.5 ft?

_____

19. What would be the scale dimensions of the entire first floor if the scale were 5 cm = 2 ft?

_____

Solve.

20. Alan wants to buy a rug for a 6 yard by 4 yard room. The rug costs $20.50 per square yard. How many square yards does he need? How much will the rug cost? _____

21. Charlene wants to put a rug in her 12 foot by 15 foot bedroom. The rug costs $18.00 per square yard. How many square yards does she need? How much will the rug cost? _____

The Mathematics of Housing and Taxes, SV 9780547625645

Decision Making: Choosing a Mortgage

Banks and other lending institutions provide many different kinds of home mortgages. Listing the features of several mortgages can help you decide which one to choose.

 TIP Try to vary only a few features of the mortgages you are comparing at one time. This makes them easier to compare without getting confused.

PROBLEM

Noel and Dave are buying a home. They need a $165,000 mortgage. They have 3 mortgages to choose from. They listed the features of each mortgage to help them decide which one to choose.

Which mortgage should Noel and Dave choose if they want:

1. the shortest term?

_____

2. the fewest closing costs?

_____

3. the lowest rate?

_____

BANKS/MORTGAGES:

1. People's Bank
Amount: $165,000
Type: fixed rate
Interest rate: 5.5%
Points: 0
Term 30 y
Other closing costs $0
APR = 5.5%

2. National Bank
Amount: $165,000
Type: Fixed Rate
Interest rate: 5.25%
Points: 3
Term: 30 y
Other closing costs: $1,200
APR = 5.59%

3. Intown Bank
Amount: $165,000
Type: Adjustable rate
Interest rate: 5%
Points: 0
Term: 20 y
Other closing costs: $850
APR = 4.789%

The Mathematics of Housing and Taxes, SV 9780547625645

Name _____ Date _____

Decision-making comparisons: Complete the table to compare the 3 mortgages. Use the Mortgage Payments table on this page to find the monthly payment.

Factors	People's Bank	National Bank	Intown Bank
Monthly payment	4. _____	5. _____	$1,089
Closing costs, including points	6. _____	$1,200 + 3% of loan amount	7. _____
Type of mortgage	Fixed	8. _____	9. _____
Term	10. _____	30 y	11. _____
Interest rate	5.5%	12. _____	13. _____
APR	5.5%	5.59%	4.789%

Mortgage rates on lenders' rate sheets normally vary in increments of 0.125%, or 1/8 of a percent as shown in the table:

MORTGAGE PAYMENTS PER $1000			
Interest Rate	Monthly Payment		
	20-y loan	25-y loan	30-y loan
5.0%	$6.60	$5.85	$5.37
5.125%	$6.67	$5.92	$5.44
5.25%	$6.74	$5.99	$5.52
5.375%	$6.81	$6.06	$5.60
5.5%	$6.88	$6.14	$5.68

Think About It

1. Why would someone ever want a mortgage with a shorter term, if the monthly payment is always higher than the same mortgage, at the same rate, over a longer term?

_____

_____

The Mathematics of Housing and Taxes, SV 9780547625645

Decision Making: "APR"

Shopping for a mortgage can be confusing. APR (Annual Percentage Rate) was developed to make things clearer. It is a calculation that tries to reflect the total costs of borrowing money. If you shop for a fixed-rate mortgage and get a slightly better rate, but you pay a lot more in closing costs to get it, you may not be getting a good deal—and APR will sometimes show this.

Think About It

1. Compare the fixed-rate loans that Noel and Dave were offered by People's Bank and National Bank. Which one has the lower monthly mortgage payment? Which one is actually more expensive?

   _____

   _____

   _____

DECISION-MAKING FACTORS:

- Monthly payment
- Closing costs, including points
- Type of mortgage
- Term (= Amount to be repaid)
- APR—annualized percentage rate

Notes:

What is APR, and why is it important?

FIXED-RATE MORTGAGES:

1. **People's Bank**
   Amount: $165,000
   Type: fixed rate
   Interest rate: 5.5%
   Points: 0
   Term 30 y
   Other closing costs $0
   APR = 5.5%

2. **National Bank**
   Amount: $165,000
   Type: Fixed Rate
   Interest rate: 5.25%
   Points: 3
   Term: 30 y
   Other closing costs: $1,200
   APR = 5.59%

Decision Making: Fixed Rate or Adjustable Rate?

Tim and Connie Cleveland want to buy a house near her family. Tim is an army officer, and he and Connie know that 3 years from now they will have to sell this house because Tim will be stationed across the country. Their loan consultant suggested that, under the circumstances, an **adjustable rate mortgage** might save them some money. Study the chart and answer the questions.

	Fixed-rate mortgage	**Adjustable-rate mortgage**
Loan amount	$165,000	$165,000
Term	30 y	30 y
Closing costs	$1,650	$0
Interest rate	5.5%, fixed for 30 y	5%, fixed for the first 3 years, then varies according to the terms of the contract, for the next 27 years

> **Adjustable Rate Mortgage (A.R.M.):** a mortgage loan subject to changes in interest rates; when rates change, ARM monthly payments increase or decrease at intervals determined by the lender; the change in monthly payment amount, however, is usually subject to a cap.

1. Which mortgage has the lower closing costs? _____

2. Which mortgage has the lower rate? _____

3. Why do you think the "cheaper" mortgage is cheaper? _____

4. Why might Tim and Connie choose an adjustable rate mortgage?

_____

_____

5. Which mortgage would you choose?

_____

Money Tips: Mortgage Rates

Mortgage rates change every day. Normally, adjustable rate mortgages carry lower rates with fewer closing costs than fixed-rate mortgages. Study the chart of a single bank on a single day. Answer the questions, based on what you have learned about mortgages.

1. Harry and Sandra want to buy a house, pay as little as possible, and keep it for 4 years. What is the best mortgage for them?

   _____

2. Carol and Ted can afford a higher monthly payment, and they want the lowest fixed rate. What should they choose?

   _____

3. Dave and Noel need a fixed-rate mortgage, but they want to keep their payment as low as possible. What loan should they get?

   _____

(Note: Notice that the APR for the adjustable rate mortgage is lower than the interest rate. The APR for adjustable rate mortgages is calculated based on the fact that its rate will vary after the fixed period (in this case, 5 years)—*and it could be lower.* APR is not a good guide when shopping for an A.R.M.)

Product	Interest rate	APR
30-Year Fixed	4.875%	5.065%
15-Year Fixed	4.250%	4.573%
5-Year ARM	3.375%	3.303%

Name _____ Date _____

When you borrow money, you pay interest for as long as you hold that money. This means that if you sign a contract for a 20-year mortgage instead of a 30-year mortgage, you pay much less interest because you are paying the money back faster. How much less? A financial calculator can tell you. Look at the results of the comparison between two very similar loans, each for $100,000. One will be paid back in 20 years; the other will be paid back in 30 years.

Study the table and answer the questions.

	20-year term	**30-year term**
Loan amount	$100,000	$100,000
Interest rate	5%	5%
Closing costs	$1,000	$1,000
Monthly payment	$660	$537
Calculation of total interest paid over life of loan	$58,389.38	$93,225.79*

*They say that, once you get done paying all the interest on a 30-year mortgage over the years that you hold it, you have essentially "bought the house twice"!

| Think About It |

1. How much more will it cost you, monthly, to assume the 20-year loan instead of the 30-year one?

   _____

2. Assume that you pay down whichever mortgage you choose, all the way to the end of the term. How much less interest will you pay, over the life of the loan, by getting the 20-year mortgage instead of the 30-year one? _____

The trade-off is that your monthly payment is higher. You need to be sure you can make the monthly payment before deciding to get a mortgage with a shorter term.

Estimation Skill: Estimations of Quotients Using Compatible Numbers

If one number can be divided by another with a remainder of 0, the numbers are called compatible numbers. You can estimate quotients using compatible numbers.

Step 1 Find compatible numbers that are close in value to the given divisor and dividend.

Step 2 Divide, using the compatible numbers.

Sometimes only the dividend needs to be changed.

Examples:	$4{,}695 \div 4$		**Examples:**	$\$93.68 \div 30$
THINK:	$4{,}800 \div 4 = 1{,}200$		**THINK:**	$\$90 \div 30 = \$3$
Estimate:	$1{,}200$		**Estimate:**	$\$3$

At other times, it is necessary to change both the divisor and the dividend.

Examples:	$372{,}568 \div 232$		**Examples:**	$762.84 \div 9.35$
THINK:	$400{,}000 \div 200 = 2{,}000$		**THINK:**	$720 \div 9 = 80$
Estimate:	$2{,}000$		**Estimate:**	80

Use compatible numbers to estimate the quotient.

1. $55 \div 3 =$ _____

2. $641 \div 2 =$ _____

3. $413 \div 4 =$ _____

4. $902 \div 32 =$ _____

5. $537 \div 61 =$ _____

6. $873 \div 22 =$ _____

7. $3892 \div 16 =$ _____

8. $85376 \div 416 =$ _____

9. $652400 \div 822 =$ _____

10. $274.62 \div 5 =$ _____

11. $31.45 \div 6 =$ _____

12. 86.38 ÷ 3 = _____

13. 912.98 ÷ 45 = _____

14. 652.30 ÷ 72= _____

15. 4362 ÷ 89 = _____

16. 185.75 ÷ 12 = _____

17. 172.30 ÷ 28 = _____

18. 4313 ÷ 22 = _____

19. 45.2 ÷ 9 = _____

20. 203.4 ÷ 7 = _____

21. 131.35 ÷ 4 = _____

22. 23 ÷ 4.2 = _____

23. 492.6 ÷ 8.1= _____

24. 30.2 ÷ 7.5 = _____

25. 0.461 ÷ 0.23 = _____

26. 28.474 ÷ 3.16 = _____

27. 29.06 ÷ 5.47 = _____

> **TIP** Compatible numbers are extremely useful when mental estimates of quotients are needed. However, there are no hard and fast rules for the procedure. For this reason, you may encounter some difficulty mastering the technique. It helps to practice your estimating skills whenever you can— in the classroom and outside it. You will be pleased to discover that, as you use the skills more and more often, they become easier to apply.

Since different pairs of compatible numbers may be chosen in many division examples, there can be multiple reasonable answers. For example, if 789.49 is divided by 9.35, either of the following estimates would be acceptable: 789.49 ÷ 9.35

THINK: 800 ÷ 10 = 80   Estimate: 80   **THINK:** 810 ÷ 9 = 90   Estimate: 90

Part III Review

Vocabulary

Choose the letter of the word(s) that complete(s) the sentence.

1. A building in which apartments are owned is called a _____.

   a. Lease   **b.** Mortgage   **c.** Condominium

2. The percent of the mortgage amount paid at the closing is called _____.

   a. Interest   **b.** Points   **c.** Appreciation

3. Utility companies sell electricity by the _____.

   a. Kilowatt hour   **b.** Cubic foot   **c.** Hour

Skills

Find the answer.

4. Ed earns $1,500 per month. What is the maximum monthly rent he should be able to afford?

   _____

5. Maria's rent is $950 per month. Her utility bill averages $150 per month. What is her average total monthly cost for these items? _____

6. Lucy earns $66,500 per year. What is the maximum that she should be able to borrow to buy a house?

   _____

7. Martin's $199,000 house appreciated 15% over the last year. What is it now worth? _____

8. Ron put 20% down on a $425,000 condo. How much was that? _____

9. Liz put 20% down on a $575,000 house. What is her mortgage amount? _____

Use the Mortgage Payments table for problems 10–11.

10. Fran got a $156,000 mortgage for 25 years at 6%. How much will she pay each month for the principal + interest ("P&I") portion of her mortgage?

_____

11. Carlos put 25% down on a $90,000 house. What are the mortgage amount and his monthly payment for a 30-year loan at 7.5%? _____

Solve.

12. Sam's mortgage was $163,000. The closing costs were 2 points and $3,260 in fees. What were his closing costs? _____

13. The market value of Monica's property is $243,000. The assessment rate is 80%. What is the assessed valuation? _____

14. Dawn's house used 2,093 kWh of electricity. How much did the electricity cost at $0.0427 per kWh?

_____

15. Diana used 172 hundred cubic feet of gas. How much did the gas cost at $0.7215 per 100 cubic feet?

_____

16. Carl's rectangular living room measures 18 feet by 21 feet by 8 feet high. How many gallons of paint are needed to paint the walls? _____

17. Miguel wants to buy a condominium with monthly payments of $643. His current gross pay is $1,875 per month. How much more would he need to earn per month to afford the condominium? _____

18. The assessed valuation of Jack's house is $245,000. The tax rate is $4.85 per $100. What is his annual real estate tax? _____

MORGAGE PAYMENTS PER $1000			
Interest Rate	Monthly Payment		
	20-y loan	25-y loan	30-y loan
5.0%	$6.60	$5.85	$5.37
5.5%	$6.88	$6.14	$5.68
6.0%	$7.16	$6.44	$6.00
6.5%	$7.46	$6.75	$6.32
7.0%	$7.75	$7.07	$6.65
7.5%	$8.06	$7.39	$6.99
8.0%	$8.36	$7.72	$7.34
8.5%	$8.68	$8.05	$7.69
9.0%	$9.00	$8.40	$8.05
9.5%	$9.33	$8.74	$8.41
10.0%	$9.66	$9.09	$8.78
10.5%	$9.99	$9.45	$9.15
11.0%	$10.33	$9.81	$9.53
11.5%	$10.66	$10.16	$9.90
12.0%	$11.01	$10.53	$10.29
12.5%	$11.36	$10.9	$10.67
13.0%	$11.72	$11.28	$11.06
13.5%	$12.07	$11.66	$11.45
14.0%	$12.44	$12.04	$11.85
14.5%	$12.80	$12.42	$12.25
15.0%	$13.17	$12.81	$12.64
15.5%	$13.54	$13.20	$13.05

Part III Test

Find the maximum monthly rent for the gross pay.

1. Gross monthly pay: $1,520 _____

2. Gross annual salary: $89,500 _____

Find the maximum to borrow for a house.

3. Gross annual income: $124,090 _____

4. Gross monthly income: $11,620 _____

Find the appreciation and the appreciated value of the house.

5. Initial value: $153,000
   Appreciation: 15% in one year

   _____

6. Initial value: $483,000
   Depreciation: –15% per y for 2 y

   _____

7. Find the total monthly cost.
   Rent: $585 per mo
   Electricity: $59 per mo
   Gas: $42 per mo
   Health club: $30 per mo

   _____

8. Find the down payment and the total monthly payment.
   Condo price: $100,980
   Maintenance: $225 per mo
   Financing: 15% down, $832 per mo

   _____

Use the Mortgage Payments table for problems 9–11.

9. What is the monthly payment on a 25-year, $295,000 mortgage at 5.25%? _____

10. What is the monthly payment on a 20-year, $350,000 mortgage at 5.375%? _____

11. What is the monthly payment on a 30-year, $220,000 mortgage at 5.5%? _____

MORTGAGE PAYMENTS PER $1000			
Interest Rate	Monthly Payment		
	20-y loan	25-y loan	30-y loan
5.0%	$6.60	$5.85	$5.37
5.125%	$6.67	$5.92	$5.44
5.25%	$6.74	$5.99	$5.52
5.375%	$6.81	$6.06	$5.60
5.5%	$6.88	$6.14	$5.68

12. The closing costs for an $183,000 mortgage were $1\frac{1}{2}$ points and $1,298 in fees. How much was that? _____

Find the assessed valuation and the annual real estate tax.

13. Market value: $230,000
Assessment rate: 80%
Tax rate: $3.29 per $100

_____

14. Market value: $198,900
Assessment rate: 75%
Tax rate: $4.09 per $100

_____

Other structure (garage, etc.):	10% of house-replacement value
Personal property:	50% of house-replacement value
Additional living expenses while house is being repaired or replaced:	20% of house-replacement value
Trees, shrubs, plants:	5% of house-replacement value

Use the information in the box for Questions 15 and 16.

15. A house is insured for its full replacement value of $137,000. What is the coverage for personal property? _____

16. John's house suffered smoke damage when there was a neighborhood fire. If the house is insured for its full replacement value of $83,500, how much will his insurance cover for him to stay elsewhere while it is being repaired? _____

Find the cost of the utility.

17. Electricity used: 3,905 kWh
Cost per kWh: $0.0398

_____

18. Water used: 4,287 cubic ft
Cost per 1,000 cubic ft: $12.97

_____

Find the answer.

19. A room measures 18 ft by 15 ft by 8 ft high. If a gallon of paint covers 400 sq. ft. (including doors and window frames), how many gallons of paint are needed to paint the walls? _____

20. How much would it cost to remodel a 22 foot by 16 foot room at $8.50 per square foot?

_____

Support Materials

Support Materials:
Group Projects

Sharing an Apartment

Today, high rents are forcing many young people into sharing an apartment. Suppose you are one of these people. You can afford to pay only $300 a month in rent and utilities. You have found a roommate who can afford to pay only $200 a month in rent and utilities. Find an apartment together by looking in local newspaper listings or by inquiring from real estate agents. How much rent will each of you be responsible for?

Questions to Think About:

1. What can you afford?
2. What neighborhoods should you consider?
3. Are utilities considered in the rent?
4. What extras—such as parking, laundry facilities, pool, and exercise room—should be considered?

What other questions do you have to think about? Make a list of these questions.

Answering the Questions

Consider how the underlying problems in each question can be a factor in determining your portion of the rent.

- Suppose you can afford only a 1-bedroom apartment. If you decide to share the bedroom, then you might want to split the rent evenly. However, if only 1 person takes the bedroom, you will probably want to split the rent differently.

- List the other expenses that might affect each person's portion of the rent. Utilities and garaging might be considered such expenses. Decide what percentage or fraction of the expenses each person will be responsible for.

Answer all the questions in your list.

Formulating and Implementing the Plan

Organize your information in a useful format and present it to the class.

- Explain how you found the apartment and why you decided on the one you have chosen.

- Explain how each person's portion of the rent was determined.

- Give reasons to support why it is a fair plan

Renovating a Classroom

Suppose your group is asked to make an estimate for renovations to your math classroom. You have a budget of $10,000. Renovations should be made to basic elements in the room, only as necessary. These include floors, walls, ceilings, windows, lighting, and so on. You can hire skilled labor, or you can do the job yourself. How would you renovate, and how much would it cost to do so?

Questions to Think About

1. What areas need renovating?

2. What materials are needed to make the renovations, and what would be the cost of these materials?

3. Is there enough in the budget to hire skilled labor?

4. What part of the renovations could you do yourself if you had to?

What other questions do you have to think about? Make a list of these questions.

Answering the Questions

One way to handle this situation is first to identify and answer the overriding questions. Determine what these questions are and then work backward from there. Two such questions might be the following:

• What elements in the classroom can be improved to make it more effective for learning?

• What is the costliest part of the renovation, and how does it affect the budget?

• When discussing these questions, you may find that the renovation is not really necessary at all, or that it doesn't have to be as extensive as you first thought.

Answer all the questions in your list. You will probably have to make compromises to come within your budget.

Formulating and Implementing the Plan

You have gathered a lot of information and have probably revised your estimates several times. Now organize your information for presentation.

• You might show a drawing that shows the elements to be renovated.

• Consider using charts or tables to show and support your recommendations.

• Present your recommendations to the class.

Support Materials:
Practice Forms

Residential Loan Application

Residential Loan Application

I. Type of Mortgage and Terms of Loan

Amount $	Interest Rate %	No. of Months	Amortization Type	☐ Fixed Rate ☐ GPM	☐ Other (explain): ☐ ARM (type):

II. Property Information and Purpose of Loan

Subject Property Address (street, city, state & ZIP)	No. of units

Legal Description of Subject Property (attach description if necessary)	Year built

Purpose of Loan ☐ Purchase ☐ Construction ☐ Other (explain): ☐ Refinance ☐ Construction-Permanent	Property will be: ☐ Primary Residence ☐ Secondary Residence ☐ Investment

Title will be in what Name(s)

III. Borrower Information

Borrower	Co-Borrower
Borrower's Name (include Jr. or Sr. if applicable)	Co-Borrower's Name (include Jr. or Sr. if applicable)

Social Security Number XXX-XX-XXXX	Home Phone (incl. area code)	Social Security Number XXX-XX-XXXX	Home Phone (incl. area code)
DOB (mm/dd/yyyy) yy/yy/yyyy	Yrs. School	DOB (mm/dd/yyyy) yy/yy/yyyy	Yrs. School
☐ Married ☐ Unmarried (include single, divorced, widowed) ☐ Separated	Dependents (not listed by Co-Borrower) no. ___ ages ___	☐ Married ☐ Unmarried (include single, divorced, widowed) ☐ Separated	Dependents (not listed by Co-Borrower) no. ___ ages ___
Present Address (street, city, state, ZIP)	☐ Own ☐ Rent No.____ Yrs.	Present Address (street, city, state, ZIP)	☐ Own ☐ Rent No.____ Yrs.
Mailing Address, if different from Present Address		Mailing Address, if different from Present Address	

IV. Employment Information

Name & Address of Employer ☐ Self Employed	Yrs. on this job	Name & Address of Employer ☐ Self Employed	Yrs. on this job
	Yrs. employed in this line of work/profession		Yrs. employed in this line of work/profession
Position/Title/Type of Business	Business Phone (incl. area code)	Position/Title/Type of Business	Business Phone (incl. area code)

Support Materials
The Mathematics of Housing and Taxes, SV 9780547625645

Residential Loan Application

V. Monthly Income and Combined Housing Expense Information

Gross Monthly Income	Borrower	Co-Borrower	Total	Combined Monthly Expenses	Present	Proposed
Base Empl. Income	$	$	$	Rent	$	
Overtime				First Mortgage (P&I)		$
Bonuses				Other Financing (P&I)		
Commissions				Hazard Insurance		
Dividends/Interest				Real Estate Taxes		
Net Rental Income				Mortgage Insurance		
Other				Homeowner Assn. Dues Other:		
Total	$	$	$	Total	$	$

VI. Asset and Liabilities

Assets Description	Cash or Market Value				
Cash deposit toward purchase held by:	$				

List checking and savings accounts below		Liabilities		Monthly Payment & Months Left to Pay	Unpaid Balance
Name and address of Bank, S&L, or Credit Union		Name and address of Bank, S&L, or Credit Union		$ Payment/Months	$
Acct. no.	$	Acct. no.	$		
Name and address of Bank, S&L, or Credit Union		Name and address of Bank, S&L, or Credit Union		$ Payment/Months	$
Acct. no.	$	Acct. no.	$		
Subtotal Liquid Assets	$				
Real estate owned (enter market value from schedule of real estate owned)	$				
		Total Monthly Payments	$		
Total Assets a.	$	Net Worth (a month)	$	Total Liabilities b.	$
Borrower's Signature X		Date	Co-Borrower's Signature X		Date

Support Materials:
Charts

Tax Table

2010 Tax Table—*Continued*

14,000

At least	But less than	Single	Married filing jointly *	Married filing separately	Head of a household
14,000	14,050	1,685	1,403	1,685	1,506
14,050	14,100	1,693	1,408	1,693	1,514
14,100	14,150	1,700	1,413	1,700	1,521
14,150	14,200	1,708	1,418	1,708	1,529
14,200	14,250	1,715	1,423	1,715	1,536
14,250	14,300	1,723	1,428	1,723	1,544
14,300	14,350	1,730	1,433	1,730	1,551
14,350	14,400	1,738	1,438	1,738	1,559
14,400	14,450	1,745	1,443	1,745	1,566
14,450	14,500	1,753	1,448	1,753	1,574
14,500	14,550	1,760	1,453	1,760	1,581
14,550	14,600	1,768	1,458	1,768	1,589
14,600	14,650	1,775	1,463	1,775	1,596
14,650	14,700	1,783	1,468	1,783	1,604
14,700	14,750	1,790	1,473	1,790	1,611
14,750	14,800	1,798	1,478	1,798	1,619
14,800	14,850	1,805	1,483	1,805	1,626
14,850	14,900	1,813	1,488	1,813	1,634
14,900	14,950	1,820	1,493	1,820	1,641
14,950	15,000	1,828	1,498	1,828	1,649

15,000

At least	But less than	Single	Married filing jointly *	Married filing separately	Head of a household
15,000	15,050	1,835	1,503	1,835	1,656
15,050	15,100	1,843	1,508	1,843	1,664
15,100	15,150	1,850	1,513	1,850	1,671
15,150	15,200	1,858	1,518	1,858	1,679
15,200	15,250	1,865	1,523	1,865	1,686
15,250	15,300	1,873	1,528	1,873	1,694
15,300	15,350	1,880	1,533	1,880	1,701
15,350	15,400	1,888	1,538	1,888	1,709
15,400	15,450	1,895	1,543	1,895	1,716
15,450	15,500	1,903	1,548	1,903	1,724
15,500	15,550	1,910	1,553	1,910	1,731
15,550	15,600	1,918	1,558	1,918	1,739
15,600	15,650	1,925	1,563	1,925	1,746
15,650	15,700	1,933	1,568	1,933	1,754
15,700	15,750	1,940	1,573	1,940	1,761
15,750	15,800	1,948	1,578	1,948	1,769
15,800	15,850	1,955	1,583	1,955	1,776
15,850	15,900	1,963	1,588	1,963	1,784
15,900	15,950	1,970	1,593	1,970	1,791
15,950	16,000	1,978	1,598	1,978	1,799

16,000

At least	But less than	Single	Married filing jointly *	Married filing separately	Head of a household
16,000	16,050	1,985	1,603	1,985	1,806
16,050	16,100	1,993	1,608	1,993	1,814
16,100	16,150	2,000	1,613	2,000	1,821
16,150	16,200	2,008	1,618	2,008	1,829
16,200	16,250	2,015	1,623	2,015	1,836
16,250	16,300	2,023	1,628	2,023	1,844
16,300	16,350	2,030	1,633	2,030	1,851
16,350	16,400	2,038	1,638	2,038	1,859
16,400	16,450	2,045	1,643	2,045	1,866
16,450	16,500	2,053	1,648	2,053	1,874
16,500	16,550	2,060	1,653	2,060	1,881
16,550	16,600	2,068	1,658	2,068	1,889
16,600	16,650	2,075	1,663	2,075	1,896
16,650	16,700	2,083	1,668	2,083	1,904
16,700	16,750	2,090	1,673	2,090	1,911
16,750	16,800	2,098	1,679	2,098	1,919
16,800	16,850	2,105	1,686	2,105	1,926
16,850	16,900	2,113	1,694	2,113	1,934
16,900	16,950	2,120	1,701	2,120	1,941
16,950	17,000	2,128	1,709	2,128	1,949

17,000

At least	But less than	Single	Married filing jointly *	Married filing separately	Head of a household
17,000	17,050	2,135	1,716	2,135	1,956
17,050	17,100	2,143	1,724	2,143	1,964
17,100	17,150	2,150	1,731	2,150	1,971
17,150	17,200	2,158	1,739	2,158	1,979
17,200	17,250	2,165	1,746	2,165	1,986
17,250	17,300	2,173	1,754	2,173	1,994
17,300	17,350	2,180	1,761	2,180	2,001
17,350	17,400	2,188	1,769	2,188	2,009
17,400	17,450	2,195	1,776	2,195	2,016
17,450	17,500	2,203	1,784	2,203	2,024
17,500	17,550	2,210	1,791	2,210	2,031
17,550	17,600	2,218	1,799	2,218	2,039
17,600	17,650	2,225	1,806	2,225	2,046
17,650	17,700	2,233	1,814	2,233	2,054
17,700	17,750	2,240	1,821	2,240	2,061
17,750	17,800	2,248	1,829	2,248	2,069
17,800	17,850	2,255	1,836	2,255	2,076
17,850	17,900	2,263	1,844	2,263	2,084
17,900	17,950	2,270	1,851	2,270	2,091
17,950	18,000	2,278	1,859	2,278	2,099

18,000

At least	But less than	Single	Married filing jointly *	Married filing separately	Head of a household
18,000	18,050	2,285	1,866	2,285	2,106
18,050	18,100	2,293	1,874	2,293	2,114
18,100	18,150	2,300	1,881	2,300	2,121
18,150	18,200	2,308	1,889	2,308	2,129
18,200	18,250	2,315	1,896	2,315	2,136
18,250	18,300	2,323	1,904	2,323	2,144
18,300	18,350	2,330	1,911	2,330	2,151
18,350	18,400	2,338	1,919	2,338	2,159
18,400	18,450	2,345	1,926	2,345	2,166
18,450	18,500	2,353	1,934	2,353	2,174
18,500	18,550	2,360	1,941	2,360	2,181
18,550	18,600	2,368	1,949	2,368	2,189
18,600	18,650	2,375	1,956	2,375	2,196
18,650	18,700	2,383	1,964	2,383	2,204
18,700	18,750	2,390	1,971	2,390	2,211
18,750	18,800	2,398	1,979	2,398	2,219
18,800	18,850	2,405	1,986	2,405	2,226
18,850	18,900	2,413	1,994	2,413	2,234
18,900	18,950	2,420	2,001	2,420	2,241
18,950	19,000	2,428	2,009	2,428	2,249

19,000

At least	But less than	Single	Married filing jointly *	Married filing separately	Head of a household
19,000	19,050	2,435	2,016	2,435	2,256
19,050	19,100	2,443	2,024	2,443	2,264
19,100	19,150	2,450	2,031	2,450	2,271
19,150	19,200	2,458	2,039	2,458	2,279
19,200	19,250	2,465	2,046	2,465	2,286
19,250	19,300	2,473	2,054	2,473	2,294
19,300	19,350	2,480	2,061	2,480	2,301
19,350	19,400	2,488	2,069	2,488	2,309
19,400	19,450	2,495	2,076	2,495	2,316
19,450	19,500	2,503	2,084	2,503	2,324
19,500	19,550	2,510	2,091	2,510	2,331
19,550	19,600	2,518	2,099	2,518	2,339
19,600	19,650	2,525	2,106	2,525	2,346
19,650	19,700	2,533	2,114	2,533	2,354
19,700	19,750	2,540	2,121	2,540	2,361
19,750	19,800	2,548	2,129	2,548	2,369
19,800	19,850	2,555	2,136	2,555	2,376
19,850	19,900	2,563	2,144	2,563	2,384
19,900	19,950	2,570	2,151	2,570	2,391
19,950	20,000	2,578	2,159	2,578	2,399

20,000

At least	But less than	Single	Married filing jointly *	Married filing separately	Head of a household
20,000	20,050	2,585	2,166	2,585	2,406
20,050	20,100	2,593	2,174	2,593	2,414
20,100	20,150	2,600	2,181	2,600	2,421
20,150	20,200	2,608	2,189	2,608	2,429
20,200	20,250	2,615	2,196	2,615	2,436
20,250	20,300	2,623	2,204	2,623	2,444
20,300	20,350	2,630	2,211	2,630	2,451
20,350	20,400	2,638	2,219	2,638	2,459
20,400	20,450	2,645	2,226	2,645	2,466
20,450	20,500	2,653	2,234	2,653	2,474
20,500	20,550	2,660	2,241	2,660	2,481
20,550	20,600	2,668	2,249	2,668	2,489
20,600	20,650	2,675	2,256	2,675	2,496
20,650	20,700	2,683	2,264	2,683	2,504
20,700	20,750	2,690	2,271	2,690	2,511
20,750	20,800	2,698	2,279	2,698	2,519
20,800	20,850	2,705	2,286	2,705	2,526
20,850	20,900	2,713	2,294	2,713	2,534
20,900	20,950	2,720	2,301	2,720	2,541
20,950	21,000	2,728	2,309	2,728	2,549

21,000

At least	But less than	Single	Married filing jointly *	Married filing separately	Head of a household
21,000	21,050	2,735	2,316	2,735	2,556
21,050	21,100	2,743	2,324	2,743	2,564
21,100	21,150	2,750	2,331	2,750	2,571
21,150	21,200	2,758	2,339	2,758	2,579
21,200	21,250	2,765	2,346	2,765	2,586
21,250	21,300	2,773	2,354	2,773	2,594
21,300	21,350	2,780	2,361	2,780	2,601
21,350	21,400	2,788	2,369	2,788	2,609
21,400	21,450	2,795	2,376	2,795	2,616
21,450	21,500	2,803	2,384	2,803	2,624
21,500	21,550	2,810	2,391	2,810	2,631
21,550	21,600	2,818	2,399	2,818	2,639
21,600	21,650	2,825	2,406	2,825	2,646
21,650	21,700	2,833	2,414	2,833	2,654
21,700	21,750	2,840	2,421	2,840	2,661
21,750	21,800	2,848	2,429	2,848	2,669
21,800	21,850	2,855	2,436	2,855	2,676
21,850	21,900	2,863	2,444	2,863	2,684
21,900	21,950	2,870	2,451	2,870	2,691
21,950	22,000	2,878	2,459	2,878	2,699

22,000

At least	But less than	Single	Married filing jointly *	Married filing separately	Head of a household
22,000	22,050	2,885	2,466	2,885	2,706
22,050	22,100	2,893	2,474	2,893	2,714
22,100	22,150	2,900	2,481	2,900	2,721
22,150	22,200	2,908	2,489	2,908	2,729
22,200	22,250	2,915	2,496	2,915	2,736
22,250	22,300	2,923	2,504	2,923	2,744
22,300	22,350	2,930	2,511	2,930	2,751
22,350	22,400	2,938	2,519	2,938	2,759
22,400	22,450	2,945	2,526	2,945	2,766
22,450	22,500	2,953	2,534	2,953	2,774
22,500	22,550	2,960	2,541	2,960	2,781
22,550	22,600	2,968	2,549	2,968	2,789
22,600	22,650	2,975	2,556	2,975	2,796
22,650	22,700	2,983	2,564	2,983	2,804
22,700	22,750	2,990	2,571	2,990	2,811
22,750	22,800	2,998	2,579	2,998	2,819
22,800	22,850	3,005	2,586	3,005	2,826
22,850	22,900	3,013	2,594	3,013	2,834
22,900	22,950	3,020	2,601	3,020	2,841
22,950	23,000	3,028	2,609	3,028	2,849

(Continued on next page)

Tax Table

If line 43 (taxable income) is—		And you are—			
At least	But less than	Single	Married filing jointly *	Married filing separately	Head of a household
		Your tax is—			
23,000					
23,000	23,050	3,035	2,616	3,035	2,856
23,050	23,100	3,043	2,624	3,043	2,864
23,100	23,150	3,050	2,631	3,050	2,871
23,150	23,200	3,058	2,639	3,058	2,879
23,200	23,250	3,065	2,646	3,065	2,886
23,250	23,300	3,073	2,654	3,073	2,894
23,300	23,350	3,080	2,661	3,080	2,901
23,350	23,400	3,088	2,669	3,088	2,909
23,400	23,450	3,095	2,676	3,095	2,916
23,450	23,500	3,103	2,684	3,103	2,924
23,500	23,550	3,110	2,691	3,110	2,931
23,550	23,600	3,118	2,699	3,118	2,939
23,600	23,650	3,125	2,706	3,125	2,946
23,650	23,700	3,133	2,714	3,133	2,954
23,700	23,750	3,140	2,721	3,140	2,961
23,750	23,800	3,148	2,729	3,148	2,969
23,800	23,850	3,155	2,736	3,155	2,976
23,850	23,900	3,163	2,744	3,163	2,984
23,900	23,950	3,170	2,751	3,170	2,991
23,950	24,000	3,178	2,759	3,178	2,999
24,000					
24,000	24,050	3,185	2,766	3,185	3,006
24,050	24,100	3,193	2,774	3,193	3,014
24,100	24,150	3,200	2,781	3,200	3,021
24,150	24,200	3,208	2,789	3,208	3,029
24,200	24,250	3,215	2,796	3,215	3,036
24,250	24,300	3,223	2,804	3,223	3,044
24,300	24,350	3,230	2,811	3,230	3,051
24,350	24,400	3,238	2,819	3,238	3,059
24,400	24,450	3,245	2,826	3,245	3,066
24,450	24,500	3,253	2,834	3,253	3,074
24,500	24,550	3,260	2,841	3,260	3,081
24,550	24,600	3,268	2,849	3,268	3,089
24,600	24,650	3,275	2,856	3,275	3,096
24,650	24,700	3,283	2,864	3,283	3,104
24,700	24,750	3,290	2,871	3,290	3,111
24,750	24,800	3,298	2,879	3,298	3,119
24,800	24,850	3,305	2,886	3,305	3,126
24,850	24,900	3,313	2,894	3,313	3,134
24,900	24,950	3,320	2,901	3,320	3,141
24,950	25,000	3,328	2,909	3,328	3,149
25,000					
25,000	25,050	3,335	2,916	3,335	3,156
25,050	25,100	3,343	2,924	3,343	3,164
25,100	25,150	3,350	2,931	3,350	3,171
25,150	25,200	3,358	2,939	3,358	3,179
25,200	25,250	3,365	2,946	3,365	3,186
25,250	25,300	3,373	2,954	3,373	3,194
25,300	25,350	3,380	2,961	3,380	3,201
25,350	25,400	3,388	2,969	3,388	3,209
25,400	25,450	3,395	2,976	3,395	3,216
25,450	25,500	3,403	2,984	3,403	3,224
25,500	25,550	3,410	2,991	3,410	3,231
25,550	25,600	3,418	2,999	3,418	3,239
25,600	25,650	3,425	3,006	3,425	3,246
25,650	25,700	3,433	3,014	3,433	3,254
25,700	25,750	3,440	3,021	3,440	3,261
25,750	25,800	3,448	3,029	3,448	3,269
25,800	25,850	3,455	3,036	3,455	3,276
25,850	25,900	3,463	3,044	3,463	3,284
25,900	25,950	3,470	3,051	3,470	3,291
25,950	26,000	3,478	3,059	3,478	3,299

If line 43 (taxable income) is—		And you are—			
At least	But less than	Single	Married filing jointly *	Married filing separately	Head of a household
		Your tax is—			
26,000					
26,000	26,050	3,485	3,066	3,485	3,306
26,050	26,100	3,493	3,074	3,493	3,314
26,100	26,150	3,500	3,081	3,500	3,321
26,150	26,200	3,508	3,089	3,508	3,329
26,200	26,250	3,515	3,096	3,515	3,336
26,250	26,300	3,523	3,104	3,523	3,344
26,300	26,350	3,530	3,111	3,530	3,351
26,350	26,400	3,538	3,119	3,538	3,359
26,400	26,450	3,545	3,126	3,545	3,366
26,450	26,500	3,553	3,134	3,553	3,374
26,500	26,550	3,560	3,141	3,560	3,381
26,550	26,600	3,568	3,149	3,568	3,389
26,600	26,650	3,575	3,156	3,575	3,396
26,650	26,700	3,583	3,164	3,583	3,404
26,700	26,750	3,590	3,171	3,590	3,411
26,750	26,800	3,598	3,179	3,598	3,419
26,800	26,850	3,605	3,186	3,605	3,426
26,850	26,900	3,613	3,194	3,613	3,434
26,900	26,950	3,620	3,201	3,620	3,441
26,950	27,000	3,628	3,209	3,628	3,449
27,000					
27,000	27,050	3,635	3,216	3,635	3,456
27,050	27,100	3,643	3,224	3,643	3,464
27,100	27,150	3,650	3,231	3,650	3,471
27,150	27,200	3,658	3,239	3,658	3,479
27,200	27,250	3,665	3,246	3,665	3,486
27,250	27,300	3,673	3,254	3,673	3,494
27,300	27,350	3,680	3,261	3,680	3,501
27,350	27,400	3,688	3,269	3,688	3,509
27,400	27,450	3,695	3,276	3,695	3,516
27,450	27,500	3,703	3,284	3,703	3,524
27,500	27,550	3,710	3,291	3,710	3,531
27,550	27,600	3,718	3,299	3,718	3,539
27,600	27,650	3,725	3,306	3,725	3,546
27,650	27,700	3,733	3,314	3,733	3,554
27,700	27,750	3,740	3,321	3,740	3,561
27,750	27,800	3,748	3,329	3,748	3,569
27,800	27,850	3,755	3,336	3,755	3,576
27,850	27,900	3,763	3,344	3,763	3,584
27,900	27,950	3,770	3,351	3,770	3,591
27,950	28,000	3,778	3,359	3,778	3,599
28,000					
28,000	28,050	3,785	3,366	3,785	3,606
28,050	28,100	3,793	3,374	3,793	3,614
28,100	28,150	3,800	3,381	3,800	3,621
28,150	28,200	3,808	3,389	3,808	3,629
28,200	28,250	3,815	3,396	3,815	3,636
28,250	28,300	3,823	3,404	3,823	3,644
28,300	28,350	3,830	3,411	3,830	3,651
28,350	28,400	3,838	3,419	3,838	3,659
28,400	28,450	3,845	3,426	3,845	3,666
28,450	28,500	3,853	3,434	3,853	3,674
28,500	28,550	3,860	3,441	3,860	3,681
28,550	28,600	3,868	3,449	3,868	3,689
28,600	28,650	3,875	3,456	3,875	3,696
28,650	28,700	3,883	3,464	3,883	3,704
28,700	28,750	3,890	3,471	3,890	3,711
28,750	28,800	3,898	3,479	3,898	3,719
28,800	28,850	3,905	3,486	3,905	3,726
28,850	28,900	3,913	3,494	3,913	3,734
28,900	28,950	3,920	3,501	3,920	3,741
28,950	29,000	3,928	3,509	3,928	3,749

If line 43 (taxable income) is—		And you are—			
At least	But less than	Single	Married filing jointly *	Married filing separately	Head of a household
		Your tax is—			
29,000					
29,000	29,050	3,935	3,516	3,935	3,756
29,050	29,100	3,943	3,524	3,943	3,764
29,100	29,150	3,950	3,531	3,950	3,771
29,150	29,200	3,958	3,539	3,958	3,779
29,200	29,250	3,965	3,546	3,965	3,786
29,250	29,300	3,973	3,554	3,973	3,794
29,300	29,350	3,980	3,561	3,980	3,801
29,350	29,400	3,988	3,569	3,988	3,809
29,400	29,450	3,995	3,576	3,995	3,816
29,450	29,500	4,003	3,584	4,003	3,824
29,500	29,550	4,010	3,591	4,010	3,831
29,550	29,600	4,018	3,599	4,018	3,839
29,600	29,650	4,025	3,606	4,025	3,846
29,650	29,700	4,033	3,614	4,033	3,854
29,700	29,750	4,040	3,621	4,040	3,861
29,750	29,800	4,048	3,629	4,048	3,869
29,800	29,850	4,055	3,636	4,055	3,876
29,850	29,900	4,063	3,644	4,063	3,884
29,900	29,950	4,070	3,651	4,070	3,891
29,950	30,000	4,078	3,659	4,078	3,899
30,000					
30,000	30,050	4,085	3,666	4,085	3,906
30,050	30,100	4,093	3,674	4,093	3,914
30,100	30,150	4,100	3,681	4,100	3,921
30,150	30,200	4,108	3,689	4,108	3,929
30,200	30,250	4,115	3,696	4,115	3,936
30,250	30,300	4,123	3,704	4,123	3,944
30,300	30,350	4,130	3,711	4,130	3,951
30,350	30,400	4,138	3,719	4,138	3,959
30,400	30,450	4,145	3,726	4,145	3,966
30,450	30,500	4,153	3,734	4,153	3,974
30,500	30,550	4,160	3,741	4,160	3,981
30,550	30,600	4,168	3,749	4,168	3,989
30,600	30,650	4,175	3,756	4,175	3,996
30,650	30,700	4,183	3,764	4,183	4,004
30,700	30,750	4,190	3,771	4,190	4,011
30,750	30,800	4,198	3,779	4,198	4,019
30,800	30,850	4,205	3,786	4,205	4,026
30,850	30,900	4,213	3,794	4,213	4,034
30,900	30,950	4,220	3,801	4,220	4,041
30,950	31,000	4,228	3,809	4,228	4,049
31,000					
31,000	31,050	4,235	3,816	4,235	4,056
31,050	31,100	4,243	3,824	4,243	4,064
31,100	31,150	4,250	3,831	4,250	4,071
31,150	31,200	4,258	3,839	4,258	4,079
31,200	31,250	4,265	3,846	4,265	4,086
31,250	31,300	4,273	3,854	4,273	4,094
31,300	31,350	4,280	3,861	4,280	4,101
31,350	31,400	4,288	3,869	4,288	4,109
31,400	31,450	4,295	3,876	4,295	4,116
31,450	31,500	4,303	3,884	4,303	4,124
31,500	31,550	4,310	3,891	4,310	4,131
31,550	31,600	4,318	3,899	4,318	4,139
31,600	31,650	4,325	3,906	4,325	4,146
31,650	31,700	4,333	3,914	4,333	4,154
31,700	31,750	4,340	3,921	4,340	4,161
31,750	31,800	4,348	3,929	4,348	4,169
31,800	31,850	4,355	3,936	4,355	4,176
31,850	31,900	4,363	3,944	4,363	4,184
31,900	31,950	4,370	3,951	4,370	4,191
31,950	32,000	4,378	3,959	4,378	4,199

* This column must also be used by a qualifying widow(er).

(Continued on next page)

Support Materials
The Mathematics of Housing and Taxes, SV 9780547625645

Tax Table

32,000

At least	But less than	Single	Married filing jointly *	Married filing separately	Head of a household
		Your tax is—			
32,000	32,050	4,385	3,966	4,385	4,206
32,050	32,100	4,393	3,974	4,393	4,214
32,100	32,150	4,400	3,981	4,400	4,221
32,150	32,200	4,408	3,989	4,408	4,229
32,200	32,250	4,415	3,996	4,415	4,236
32,250	32,300	4,423	4,004	4,423	4,244
32,300	32,350	4,430	4,011	4,430	4,251
32,350	32,400	4,438	4,019	4,438	4,259
32,400	32,450	4,445	4,026	4,445	4,266
32,450	32,500	4,453	4,034	4,453	4,274
32,500	32,550	4,460	4,041	4,460	4,281
32,550	32,600	4,468	4,049	4,468	4,289
32,600	32,650	4,475	4,056	4,475	4,296
32,650	32,700	4,483	4,064	4,483	4,304
32,700	32,750	4,490	4,071	4,490	4,311
32,750	32,800	4,498	4,079	4,498	4,319
32,800	32,850	4,505	4,086	4,505	4,326
32,850	32,900	4,513	4,094	4,513	4,334
32,900	32,950	4,520	4,101	4,520	4,341
32,950	33,000	4,528	4,109	4,528	4,349

33,000

At least	But less than	Single	Married filing jointly *	Married filing separately	Head of a household
33,000	33,050	4,535	4,116	4,535	4,356
33,050	33,100	4,543	4,124	4,543	4,364
33,100	33,150	4,550	4,131	4,550	4,371
33,150	33,200	4,558	4,139	4,558	4,379
33,200	33,250	4,565	4,146	4,565	4,386
33,250	33,300	4,573	4,154	4,573	4,394
33,300	33,350	4,580	4,161	4,580	4,401
33,350	33,400	4,588	4,169	4,588	4,409
33,400	33,450	4,595	4,176	4,595	4,416
33,450	33,500	4,603	4,184	4,603	4,424
33,500	33,550	4,610	4,191	4,610	4,431
33,550	33,600	4,618	4,199	4,618	4,439
33,600	33,650	4,625	4,206	4,625	4,446
33,650	33,700	4,633	4,214	4,633	4,454
33,700	33,750	4,640	4,221	4,640	4,461
33,750	33,800	4,648	4,229	4,648	4,469
33,800	33,850	4,655	4,236	4,655	4,476
33,850	33,900	4,663	4,244	4,663	4,484
33,900	33,950	4,670	4,251	4,670	4,491
33,950	34,000	4,678	4,259	4,678	4,499

34,000

At least	But less than	Single	Married filing jointly *	Married filing separately	Head of a household
34,000	34,050	4,688	4,266	4,688	4,506
34,050	34,100	4,700	4,274	4,700	4,514
34,100	34,150	4,713	4,281	4,713	4,521
34,150	34,200	4,725	4,289	4,725	4,529
34,200	34,250	4,738	4,296	4,738	4,536
34,250	34,300	4,750	4,304	4,750	4,544
34,300	34,350	4,763	4,311	4,763	4,551
34,350	34,400	4,775	4,319	4,775	4,559
34,400	34,450	4,788	4,326	4,788	4,566
34,450	34,500	4,800	4,334	4,800	4,574
34,500	34,550	4,813	4,341	4,813	4,581
34,550	34,600	4,825	4,349	4,825	4,589
34,600	34,650	4,838	4,356	4,838	4,596
34,650	34,700	4,850	4,364	4,850	4,604
34,700	34,750	4,863	4,371	4,863	4,611
34,750	34,800	4,875	4,379	4,875	4,619
34,800	34,850	4,888	4,386	4,888	4,626
34,850	34,900	4,900	4,394	4,900	4,634
34,900	34,950	4,913	4,401	4,913	4,641
34,950	35,000	4,925	4,409	4,925	4,649

35,000

At least	But less than	Single	Married filing jointly *	Married filing separately	Head of a household
35,000	35,050	4,938	4,416	4,938	4,656
35,050	35,100	4,950	4,424	4,950	4,664
35,100	35,150	4,963	4,431	4,963	4,671
35,150	35,200	4,975	4,439	4,975	4,679
35,200	35,250	4,988	4,446	4,988	4,686
35,250	35,300	5,000	4,454	5,000	4,694
35,300	35,350	5,013	4,461	5,013	4,701
35,350	35,400	5,025	4,469	5,025	4,709
35,400	35,450	5,038	4,476	5,038	4,716
35,450	35,500	5,050	4,484	5,050	4,724
35,500	35,550	5,063	4,491	5,063	4,731
35,550	35,600	5,075	4,499	5,075	4,739
35,600	35,650	5,088	4,506	5,088	4,746
35,650	35,700	5,100	4,514	5,100	4,754
35,700	35,750	5,113	4,521	5,113	4,761
35,750	35,800	5,125	4,529	5,125	4,769
35,800	35,850	5,138	4,536	5,138	4,776
35,850	35,900	5,150	4,544	5,150	4,784
35,900	35,950	5,163	4,551	5,163	4,791
35,950	36,000	5,175	4,559	5,175	4,799

36,000

At least	But less than	Single	Married filing jointly *	Married filing separately	Head of a household
36,000	36,050	5,188	4,566	5,188	4,806
36,050	36,100	5,200	4,574	5,200	4,814
36,100	36,150	5,213	4,581	5,213	4,821
36,150	36,200	5,225	4,589	5,225	4,829
36,200	36,250	5,238	4,596	5,238	4,836
36,250	36,300	5,250	4,604	5,250	4,844
36,300	36,350	5,263	4,611	5,263	4,851
36,350	36,400	5,275	4,619	5,275	4,859
36,400	36,450	5,288	4,626	5,288	4,866
36,450	36,500	5,300	4,634	5,300	4,874
36,500	36,550	5,313	4,641	5,313	4,881
36,550	36,600	5,325	4,649	5,325	4,889
36,600	36,650	5,338	4,656	5,338	4,896
36,650	36,700	5,350	4,664	5,350	4,904
36,700	36,750	5,363	4,671	5,363	4,911
36,750	36,800	5,375	4,679	5,375	4,919
36,800	36,850	5,388	4,686	5,388	4,926
36,850	36,900	5,400	4,694	5,400	4,934
36,900	36,950	5,413	4,701	5,413	4,941
36,950	37,000	5,425	4,709	5,425	4,949

37,000

At least	But less than	Single	Married filing jointly *	Married filing separately	Head of a household
37,000	37,050	5,438	4,716	5,438	4,956
37,050	37,100	5,450	4,724	5,450	4,964
37,100	37,150	5,463	4,731	5,463	4,971
37,150	37,200	5,475	4,739	5,475	4,979
37,200	37,250	5,488	4,746	5,488	4,986
37,250	37,300	5,500	4,754	5,500	4,994
37,300	37,350	5,513	4,761	5,513	5,001
37,350	37,400	5,525	4,769	5,525	5,009
37,400	37,450	5,538	4,776	5,538	5,016
37,450	37,500	5,550	4,784	5,550	5,024
37,500	37,550	5,563	4,791	5,563	5,031
37,550	37,600	5,575	4,799	5,575	5,039
37,600	37,650	5,588	4,806	5,588	5,046
37,650	37,700	5,600	4,814	5,600	5,054
37,700	37,750	5,613	4,821	5,613	5,061
37,750	37,800	5,625	4,829	5,625	5,069
37,800	37,850	5,638	4,836	5,638	5,076
37,850	37,900	5,650	4,844	5,650	5,084
37,900	37,950	5,663	4,851	5,663	5,091
37,950	38,000	5,675	4,859	5,675	5,099

38,000

At least	But less than	Single	Married filing jointly *	Married filing separately	Head of a household
38,000	38,050	5,688	4,866	5,688	5,106
38,050	38,100	5,700	4,874	5,700	5,114
38,100	38,150	5,713	4,881	5,713	5,121
38,150	38,200	5,725	4,889	5,725	5,129
38,200	38,250	5,738	4,896	5,738	5,136
38,250	38,300	5,750	4,904	5,750	5,144
38,300	38,350	5,763	4,911	5,763	5,151
38,350	38,400	5,775	4,919	5,775	5,159
38,400	38,450	5,788	4,926	5,788	5,166
38,450	38,500	5,800	4,934	5,800	5,174
38,500	38,550	5,813	4,941	5,813	5,181
38,550	38,600	5,825	4,949	5,825	5,189
38,600	38,650	5,838	4,956	5,838	5,196
38,650	38,700	5,850	4,964	5,850	5,204
38,700	38,750	5,863	4,971	5,863	5,211
38,750	38,800	5,875	4,979	5,875	5,219
38,800	38,850	5,888	4,986	5,888	5,226
38,850	38,900	5,900	4,994	5,900	5,234
38,900	38,950	5,913	5,001	5,913	5,241
38,950	39,000	5,925	5,009	5,925	5,249

39,000

At least	But less than	Single	Married filing jointly *	Married filing separately	Head of a household
39,000	39,050	5,938	5,016	5,938	5,256
39,050	39,100	5,950	5,024	5,950	5,264
39,100	39,150	5,963	5,031	5,963	5,271
39,150	39,200	5,975	5,039	5,975	5,279
39,200	39,250	5,988	5,046	5,988	5,286
39,250	39,300	6,000	5,054	6,000	5,294
39,300	39,350	6,013	5,061	6,013	5,301
39,350	39,400	6,025	5,069	6,025	5,309
39,400	39,450	6,038	5,076	6,038	5,316
39,450	39,500	6,050	5,084	6,050	5,324
39,500	39,550	6,063	5,091	6,063	5,331
39,550	39,600	6,075	5,099	6,075	5,339
39,600	39,650	6,088	5,106	6,088	5,346
39,650	39,700	6,100	5,114	6,100	5,354
39,700	39,750	6,113	5,121	6,113	5,361
39,750	39,800	6,125	5,129	6,125	5,369
39,800	39,850	6,138	5,136	6,138	5,376
39,850	39,900	6,150	5,144	6,150	5,384
39,900	39,950	6,163	5,151	6,163	5,391
39,950	40,000	6,175	5,159	6,175	5,399

40,000

At least	But less than	Single	Married filing jointly *	Married filing separately	Head of a household
40,000	40,050	6,188	5,166	6,188	5,406
40,050	40,100	6,200	5,174	6,200	5,414
40,100	40,150	6,213	5,181	6,213	5,421
40,150	40,200	6,225	5,189	6,225	5,429
40,200	40,250	6,238	5,196	6,238	5,436
40,250	40,300	6,250	5,204	6,250	5,444
40,300	40,350	6,263	5,211	6,263	5,451
40,350	40,400	6,275	5,219	6,275	5,459
40,400	40,450	6,288	5,226	6,288	5,466
40,450	40,500	6,300	5,234	6,300	5,474
40,500	40,550	6,313	5,241	6,313	5,481
40,550	40,600	6,325	5,249	6,325	5,489
40,600	40,650	6,338	5,256	6,338	5,496
40,650	40,700	6,350	5,264	6,350	5,504
40,700	40,750	6,363	5,271	6,363	5,511
40,750	40,800	6,375	5,279	6,375	5,519
40,800	40,850	6,388	5,286	6,388	5,526
40,850	40,900	6,400	5,294	6,400	5,534
40,900	40,950	6,413	5,301	6,413	5,541
40,950	41,000	6,425	5,309	6,425	5,549

* This column must also be used by a qualifying widow(er).

(Continued on next page)

Tax Table

If line 43 (taxable income) is—		And you are—			
At least	But less than	Single	Married filing jointly *	Married filing separately	Head of a household
		Your tax is—			

41,000

At least	But less than	Single	Married filing jointly	Married filing separately	Head of household
41,000	41,050	6,438	5,316	6,438	5,556
41,050	41,100	6,450	5,324	6,450	5,564
41,100	41,150	6,463	5,331	6,463	5,571
41,150	41,200	6,475	5,339	6,475	5,579
41,200	41,250	6,488	5,346	6,488	5,586
41,250	41,300	6,500	5,354	6,500	5,594
41,300	41,350	6,513	5,361	6,513	5,601
41,350	41,400	6,525	5,369	6,525	5,609
41,400	41,450	6,538	5,376	6,538	5,616
41,450	41,500	6,550	5,384	6,550	5,624
41,500	41,550	6,563	5,391	6,563	5,631
41,550	41,600	6,575	5,399	6,575	5,639
41,600	41,650	6,588	5,406	6,588	5,646
41,650	41,700	6,600	5,414	6,600	5,654
41,700	41,750	6,613	5,421	6,613	5,661
41,750	41,800	6,625	5,429	6,625	5,669
41,800	41,850	6,638	5,436	6,638	5,676
41,850	41,900	6,650	5,444	6,650	5,684
41,900	41,950	6,663	5,451	6,663	5,691
41,950	42,000	6,675	5,459	6,675	5,699

42,000

At least	But less than	Single	Married filing jointly	Married filing separately	Head of household
42,000	42,050	6,688	5,466	6,688	5,706
42,050	42,100	6,700	5,474	6,700	5,714
42,100	42,150	6,713	5,481	6,713	5,721
42,150	42,200	6,725	5,489	6,725	5,729
42,200	42,250	6,738	5,496	6,738	5,736
42,250	42,300	6,750	5,504	6,750	5,744
42,300	42,350	6,763	5,511	6,763	5,751
42,350	42,400	6,775	5,519	6,775	5,759
42,400	42,450	6,788	5,526	6,788	5,766
42,450	42,500	6,800	5,534	6,800	5,774
42,500	42,550	6,813	5,541	6,813	5,781
42,550	42,600	6,825	5,549	6,825	5,789
42,600	42,650	6,838	5,556	6,838	5,796
42,650	42,700	6,850	5,564	6,850	5,804
42,700	42,750	6,863	5,571	6,863	5,811
42,750	42,800	6,875	5,579	6,875	5,819
42,800	42,850	6,888	5,586	6,888	5,826
42,850	42,900	6,900	5,594	6,900	5,834
42,900	42,950	6,913	5,601	6,913	5,841
42,950	43,000	6,925	5,609	6,925	5,849

43,000

At least	But less than	Single	Married filing jointly	Married filing separately	Head of household
43,000	43,050	6,938	5,616	6,938	5,856
43,050	43,100	6,950	5,624	6,950	5,864
43,100	43,150	6,963	5,631	6,963	5,871
43,150	43,200	6,975	5,639	6,975	5,879
43,200	43,250	6,988	5,646	6,988	5,886
43,250	43,300	7,000	5,654	7,000	5,894
43,300	43,350	7,013	5,661	7,013	5,901
43,350	43,400	7,025	5,669	7,025	5,909
43,400	43,450	7,038	5,676	7,038	5,916
43,450	43,500	7,050	5,684	7,050	5,924
43,500	43,550	7,063	5,691	7,063	5,931
43,550	43,600	7,075	5,699	7,075	5,939
43,600	43,650	7,088	5,706	7,088	5,946
43,650	43,700	7,100	5,714	7,100	5,954
43,700	43,750	7,113	5,721	7,113	5,961
43,750	43,800	7,125	5,729	7,125	5,969
43,800	43,850	7,138	5,736	7,138	5,976
43,850	43,900	7,150	5,744	7,150	5,984
43,900	43,950	7,163	5,751	7,163	5,991
43,950	44,000	7,175	5,759	7,175	5,999

44,000

At least	But less than	Single	Married filing jointly	Married filing separately	Head of household
44,000	44,050	7,188	5,766	7,188	6,006
44,050	44,100	7,200	5,774	7,200	6,014
44,100	44,150	7,213	5,781	7,213	6,021
44,150	44,200	7,225	5,789	7,225	6,029
44,200	44,250	7,238	5,796	7,238	6,036
44,250	44,300	7,250	5,804	7,250	6,044
44,300	44,350	7,263	5,811	7,263	6,051
44,350	44,400	7,275	5,819	7,275	6,059
44,400	44,450	7,288	5,826	7,288	6,066
44,450	44,500	7,300	5,834	7,300	6,074
44,500	44,550	7,313	5,841	7,313	6,081
44,550	44,600	7,325	5,849	7,325	6,089
44,600	44,650	7,338	5,856	7,338	6,096
44,650	44,700	7,350	5,864	7,350	6,104
44,700	44,750	7,363	5,871	7,363	6,111
44,750	44,800	7,375	5,879	7,375	6,119
44,800	44,850	7,388	5,886	7,388	6,126
44,850	44,900	7,400	5,894	7,400	6,134
44,900	44,950	7,413	5,901	7,413	6,141
44,950	45,000	7,425	5,909	7,425	6,149

45,000

At least	But less than	Single	Married filing jointly	Married filing separately	Head of household
45,000	45,050	7,438	5,916	7,438	6,156
45,050	45,100	7,450	5,924	7,450	6,164
45,100	45,150	7,463	5,931	7,463	6,171
45,150	45,200	7,475	5,939	7,475	6,179
45,200	45,250	7,488	5,946	7,488	6,186
45,250	45,300	7,500	5,954	7,500	6,194
45,300	45,350	7,513	5,961	7,513	6,201
45,350	45,400	7,525	5,969	7,525	6,209
45,400	45,450	7,538	5,976	7,538	6,216
45,450	45,500	7,550	5,984	7,550	6,224
45,500	45,550	7,563	5,991	7,563	6,231
45,550	45,600	7,575	5,999	7,575	6,241
45,600	45,650	7,588	6,006	7,588	6,254
45,650	45,700	7,600	6,014	7,600	6,266
45,700	45,750	7,613	6,021	7,613	6,279
45,750	45,800	7,625	6,029	7,625	6,291
45,800	45,850	7,638	6,036	7,638	6,304
45,850	45,900	7,650	6,044	7,650	6,316
45,900	45,950	7,663	6,051	7,663	6,329
45,950	46,000	7,675	6,059	7,675	6,341

46,000

At least	But less than	Single	Married filing jointly	Married filing separately	Head of household
46,000	46,050	7,688	6,066	7,688	6,354
46,050	46,100	7,700	6,074	7,700	6,366
46,100	46,150	7,713	6,081	7,713	6,379
46,150	46,200	7,725	6,089	7,725	6,391
46,200	46,250	7,738	6,096	7,738	6,404
46,250	46,300	7,750	6,104	7,750	6,416
46,300	46,350	7,763	6,111	7,763	6,429
46,350	46,400	7,775	6,119	7,775	6,441
46,400	46,450	7,788	6,126	7,788	6,454
46,450	46,500	7,800	6,134	7,800	6,466
46,500	46,550	7,813	6,141	7,813	6,479
46,550	46,600	7,825	6,149	7,825	6,491
46,600	46,650	7,838	6,156	7,838	6,504
46,650	46,700	7,850	6,164	7,850	6,516
46,700	46,750	7,863	6,171	7,863	6,529
46,750	46,800	7,875	6,179	7,875	6,541
46,800	46,850	7,888	6,186	7,888	6,554
46,850	46,900	7,900	6,194	7,900	6,566
46,900	46,950	7,913	6,201	7,913	6,579
46,950	47,000	7,925	6,209	7,925	6,591

47,000

At least	But less than	Single	Married filing jointly	Married filing separately	Head of household
47,000	47,050	7,938	6,216	7,938	6,604
47,050	47,100	7,950	6,224	7,950	6,616
47,100	47,150	7,963	6,231	7,963	6,629
47,150	47,200	7,975	6,239	7,975	6,641
47,200	47,250	7,988	6,246	7,988	6,654
47,250	47,300	8,000	6,254	8,000	6,666
47,300	47,350	8,013	6,261	8,013	6,679
47,350	47,400	8,025	6,269	8,025	6,691
47,400	47,450	8,038	6,276	8,038	6,704
47,450	47,500	8,050	6,284	8,050	6,716
47,500	47,550	8,063	6,291	8,063	6,729
47,550	47,600	8,075	6,299	8,075	6,741
47,600	47,650	8,088	6,306	8,088	6,754
47,650	47,700	8,100	6,314	8,100	6,766
47,700	47,750	8,113	6,321	8,113	6,779
47,750	47,800	8,125	6,329	8,125	6,791
47,800	47,850	8,138	6,336	8,138	6,804
47,850	47,900	8,150	6,344	8,150	6,816
47,900	47,950	8,163	6,351	8,163	6,829
47,950	48,000	8,175	6,359	8,175	6,841

48,000

At least	But less than	Single	Married filing jointly	Married filing separately	Head of household
48,000	48,050	8,188	6,366	8,188	6,854
48,050	48,100	8,200	6,374	8,200	6,866
48,100	48,150	8,213	6,381	8,213	6,879
48,150	48,200	8,225	6,389	8,225	6,891
48,200	48,250	8,238	6,396	8,238	6,904
48,250	48,300	8,250	6,404	8,250	6,916
48,300	48,350	8,263	6,411	8,263	6,929
48,350	48,400	8,275	6,419	8,275	6,941
48,400	48,450	8,288	6,426	8,288	6,954
48,450	48,500	8,300	6,434	8,300	6,966
48,500	48,550	8,313	6,441	8,313	6,979
48,550	48,600	8,325	6,449	8,325	6,991
48,600	48,650	8,338	6,456	8,338	7,004
48,650	48,700	8,350	6,464	8,350	7,016
48,700	48,750	8,363	6,471	8,363	7,029
48,750	48,800	8,375	6,479	8,375	7,041
48,800	48,850	8,388	6,486	8,388	7,054
48,850	48,900	8,400	6,494	8,400	7,066
48,900	48,950	8,413	6,501	8,413	7,079
48,950	49,000	8,425	6,509	8,425	7,091

49,000

At least	But less than	Single	Married filing jointly	Married filing separately	Head of household
49,000	49,050	8,438	6,516	8,438	7,104
49,050	49,100	8,450	6,524	8,450	7,116
49,100	49,150	8,463	6,531	8,463	7,129
49,150	49,200	8,475	6,539	8,475	7,141
49,200	49,250	8,488	6,546	8,488	7,154
49,250	49,300	8,500	6,554	8,500	7,166
49,300	49,350	8,513	6,561	8,513	7,179
49,350	49,400	8,525	6,569	8,525	7,191
49,400	49,450	8,538	6,576	8,538	7,204
49,450	49,500	8,550	6,584	8,550	7,216
49,500	49,550	8,563	6,591	8,563	7,229
49,550	49,600	8,575	6,599	8,575	7,241
49,600	49,650	8,588	6,606	8,588	7,254
49,650	49,700	8,600	6,614	8,600	7,266
49,700	49,750	8,613	6,621	8,613	7,279
49,750	49,800	8,625	6,629	8,625	7,291
49,800	49,850	8,638	6,636	8,638	7,304
49,850	49,900	8,650	6,644	8,650	7,316
49,900	49,950	8,663	6,651	8,663	7,329
49,950	50,000	8,675	6,659	8,675	7,341

* This column must also be used by a qualifying widow(er).

(Continued on next page)

Support Materials
The Mathematics of Housing and Taxes, SV 9780547625645

Tax Table

2010 Tax Table—Continued

If line 43 (taxable income) is— / And you are—

At least	But less than	Single	Married filing jointly *	Married filing separately	Head of a household
50,000					
50,000	50,050	8,688	6,666	8,688	7,354
50,050	50,100	8,700	6,674	8,700	7,366
50,100	50,150	8,713	6,681	8,713	7,379
50,150	50,200	8,725	6,689	8,725	7,391
50,200	50,250	8,738	6,696	8,738	7,404
50,250	50,300	8,750	6,704	8,750	7,416
50,300	50,350	8,763	6,711	8,763	7,429
50,350	50,400	8,775	6,719	8,775	7,441
50,400	50,450	8,788	6,726	8,788	7,454
50,450	50,500	8,800	6,734	8,800	7,466
50,500	50,550	8,813	6,741	8,813	7,479
50,550	50,600	8,825	6,749	8,825	7,491
50,600	50,650	8,838	6,756	8,838	7,504
50,650	50,700	8,850	6,764	8,850	7,516
50,700	50,750	8,863	6,771	8,863	7,529
50,750	50,800	8,875	6,779	8,875	7,541
50,800	50,850	8,888	6,786	8,888	7,554
50,850	50,900	8,900	6,794	8,900	7,566
50,900	50,950	8,913	6,801	8,913	7,579
50,950	51,000	8,925	6,809	8,925	7,591
51,000					
51,000	51,050	8,938	6,816	8,938	7,604
51,050	51,100	8,950	6,824	8,950	7,616
51,100	51,150	8,963	6,831	8,963	7,629
51,150	51,200	8,975	6,839	8,975	7,641
51,200	51,250	8,988	6,846	8,988	7,654
51,250	51,300	9,000	6,854	9,000	7,666
51,300	51,350	9,013	6,861	9,013	7,679
51,350	51,400	9,025	6,869	9,025	7,691
51,400	51,450	9,038	6,876	9,038	7,704
51,450	51,500	9,050	6,884	9,050	7,716
51,500	51,550	9,063	6,891	9,063	7,729
51,550	51,600	9,075	6,899	9,075	7,741
51,600	51,650	9,088	6,906	9,088	7,754
51,650	51,700	9,100	6,914	9,100	7,766
51,700	51,750	9,113	6,921	9,113	7,779
51,750	51,800	9,125	6,929	9,125	7,791
51,800	51,850	9,138	6,936	9,138	7,804
51,850	51,900	9,150	6,944	9,150	7,816
51,900	51,950	9,163	6,951	9,163	7,829
51,950	52,000	9,175	6,959	9,175	7,841
52,000					
52,000	52,050	9,188	6,966	9,188	7,854
52,050	52,100	9,200	6,974	9,200	7,866
52,100	52,150	9,213	6,981	9,213	7,879
52,150	52,200	9,225	6,989	9,225	7,891
52,200	52,250	9,238	6,996	9,238	7,904
52,250	52,300	9,250	7,004	9,250	7,916
52,300	52,350	9,263	7,011	9,263	7,929
52,350	52,400	9,275	7,019	9,275	7,941
52,400	52,450	9,288	7,026	9,288	7,954
52,450	52,500	9,300	7,034	9,300	7,966
52,500	52,550	9,313	7,041	9,313	7,979
52,550	52,600	9,325	7,049	9,325	7,991
52,600	52,650	9,338	7,056	9,338	8,004
52,650	52,700	9,350	7,064	9,350	8,016
52,700	52,750	9,363	7,071	9,363	8,029
52,750	52,800	9,375	7,079	9,375	8,041
52,800	52,850	9,388	7,086	9,388	8,054
52,850	52,900	9,400	7,094	9,400	8,066
52,900	52,950	9,413	7,101	9,413	8,079
52,950	53,000	9,425	7,109	9,425	8,091

If line 43 (taxable income) is— / And you are—

At least	But less than	Single	Married filing jointly *	Married filing separately	Head of a household
53,000					
53,000	53,050	9,438	7,116	9,438	8,104
53,050	53,100	9,450	7,124	9,450	8,116
53,100	53,150	9,463	7,131	9,463	8,129
53,150	53,200	9,475	7,139	9,475	8,141
53,200	53,250	9,488	7,146	9,488	8,154
53,250	53,300	9,500	7,154	9,500	8,166
53,300	53,350	9,513	7,161	9,513	8,179
53,350	53,400	9,525	7,169	9,525	8,191
53,400	53,450	9,538	7,176	9,538	8,204
53,450	53,500	9,550	7,184	9,550	8,216
53,500	53,550	9,563	7,191	9,563	8,229
53,550	53,600	9,575	7,199	9,575	8,241
53,600	53,650	9,588	7,206	9,588	8,254
53,650	53,700	9,600	7,214	9,600	8,266
53,700	53,750	9,613	7,221	9,613	8,279
53,750	53,800	9,625	7,229	9,625	8,291
53,800	53,850	9,638	7,236	9,638	8,304
53,850	53,900	9,650	7,244	9,650	8,316
53,900	53,950	9,663	7,251	9,663	8,329
53,950	54,000	9,675	7,259	9,675	8,341
54,000					
54,000	54,050	9,688	7,266	9,688	8,354
54,050	54,100	9,700	7,274	9,700	8,366
54,100	54,150	9,713	7,281	9,713	8,379
54,150	54,200	9,725	7,289	9,725	8,391
54,200	54,250	9,738	7,296	9,738	8,404
54,250	54,300	9,750	7,304	9,750	8,416
54,300	54,350	9,763	7,311	9,763	8,429
54,350	54,400	9,775	7,319	9,775	8,441
54,400	54,450	9,788	7,326	9,788	8,454
54,450	54,500	9,800	7,334	9,800	8,466
54,500	54,550	9,813	7,341	9,813	8,479
54,550	54,600	9,825	7,349	9,825	8,491
54,600	54,650	9,838	7,356	9,838	8,504
54,650	54,700	9,850	7,364	9,850	8,516
54,700	54,750	9,863	7,371	9,863	8,529
54,750	54,800	9,875	7,379	9,875	8,541
54,800	54,850	9,888	7,386	9,888	8,554
54,850	54,900	9,900	7,394	9,900	8,566
54,900	54,950	9,913	7,401	9,913	8,579
54,950	55,000	9,925	7,409	9,925	8,591
55,000					
55,000	55,050	9,938	7,416	9,938	8,604
55,050	55,100	9,950	7,424	9,950	8,616
55,100	55,150	9,963	7,431	9,963	8,629
55,150	55,200	9,975	7,439	9,975	8,641
55,200	55,250	9,988	7,446	9,988	8,654
55,250	55,300	10,000	7,454	10,000	8,666
55,300	55,350	10,013	7,461	10,013	8,679
55,350	55,400	10,025	7,469	10,025	8,691
55,400	55,450	10,038	7,476	10,038	8,704
55,450	55,500	10,050	7,484	10,050	8,716
55,500	55,550	10,063	7,491	10,063	8,729
55,550	55,600	10,075	7,499	10,075	8,741
55,600	55,650	10,088	7,506	10,088	8,754
55,650	55,700	10,100	7,514	10,100	8,766
55,700	55,750	10,113	7,521	10,113	8,779
55,750	55,800	10,125	7,529	10,125	8,791
55,800	55,850	10,138	7,536	10,138	8,804
55,850	55,900	10,150	7,544	10,150	8,816
55,900	55,950	10,163	7,551	10,163	8,829
55,950	56,000	10,175	7,559	10,175	8,841

If line 43 (taxable income) is— / And you are—

At least	But less than	Single	Married filing jointly *	Married filing separately	Head of a household
56,000					
56,000	56,050	10,188	7,566	10,188	8,854
56,050	56,100	10,200	7,574	10,200	8,866
56,100	56,150	10,213	7,581	10,213	8,879
56,150	56,200	10,225	7,589	10,225	8,891
56,200	56,250	10,238	7,596	10,238	8,904
56,250	56,300	10,250	7,604	10,250	8,916
56,300	56,350	10,263	7,611	10,263	8,929
56,350	56,400	10,275	7,619	10,275	8,941
56,400	56,450	10,288	7,626	10,288	8,954
56,450	56,500	10,300	7,634	10,300	8,966
56,500	56,550	10,313	7,641	10,313	8,979
56,550	56,600	10,325	7,649	10,325	8,991
56,600	56,650	10,338	7,656	10,338	9,004
56,650	56,700	10,350	7,664	10,350	9,016
56,700	56,750	10,363	7,671	10,363	9,029
56,750	56,800	10,375	7,679	10,375	9,041
56,800	56,850	10,388	7,686	10,388	9,054
56,850	56,900	10,400	7,694	10,400	9,066
56,900	56,950	10,413	7,701	10,413	9,079
56,950	57,000	10,425	7,709	10,425	9,091
57,000					
57,000	57,050	10,438	7,716	10,438	9,104
57,050	57,100	10,450	7,724	10,450	9,116
57,100	57,150	10,463	7,731	10,463	9,129
57,150	57,200	10,475	7,739	10,475	9,141
57,200	57,250	10,488	7,746	10,488	9,154
57,250	57,300	10,500	7,754	10,500	9,166
57,300	57,350	10,513	7,761	10,513	9,179
57,350	57,400	10,525	7,769	10,525	9,191
57,400	57,450	10,538	7,776	10,538	9,204
57,450	57,500	10,550	7,784	10,550	9,216
57,500	57,550	10,563	7,791	10,563	9,229
57,550	57,600	10,575	7,799	10,575	9,241
57,600	57,650	10,588	7,806	10,588	9,254
57,650	57,700	10,600	7,814	10,600	9,266
57,700	57,750	10,613	7,821	10,613	9,279
57,750	57,800	10,625	7,829	10,625	9,291
57,800	57,850	10,638	7,836	10,638	9,304
57,850	57,900	10,650	7,844	10,650	9,316
57,900	57,950	10,663	7,851	10,663	9,329
57,950	58,000	10,675	7,859	10,675	9,341
58,000					
58,000	58,050	10,688	7,866	10,688	9,354
58,050	58,100	10,700	7,874	10,700	9,366
58,100	58,150	10,713	7,881	10,713	9,379
58,150	58,200	10,725	7,889	10,725	9,391
58,200	58,250	10,738	7,896	10,738	9,404
58,250	58,300	10,750	7,904	10,750	9,416
58,300	58,350	10,763	7,911	10,763	9,429
58,350	58,400	10,775	7,919	10,775	9,441
58,400	58,450	10,788	7,926	10,788	9,454
58,450	58,500	10,800	7,934	10,800	9,466
58,500	58,550	10,813	7,941	10,813	9,479
58,550	58,600	10,825	7,949	10,825	9,491
58,600	58,650	10,838	7,956	10,838	9,504
58,650	58,700	10,850	7,964	10,850	9,516
58,700	58,750	10,863	7,971	10,863	9,529
58,750	58,800	10,875	7,979	10,875	9,541
58,800	58,850	10,888	7,986	10,888	9,554
58,850	58,900	10,900	7,994	10,900	9,566
58,900	58,950	10,913	8,001	10,913	9,579
58,950	59,000	10,925	8,009	10,925	9,591

* This column must also be used by a qualifying widow(er).

(Continued on next page)

Support Materials
The Mathematics of Housing and Taxes, SV 9780547625645

Tax Table

At least	But less than	Single	Married filing jointly *	Married filing separately	Head of a household
59,000					
59,000	59,050	10,938	8,016	10,938	9,604
59,050	59,100	10,950	8,024	10,950	9,616
59,100	59,150	10,963	8,031	10,963	9,629
59,150	59,200	10,975	8,039	10,975	9,641
59,200	59,250	10,988	8,046	10,988	9,654
59,250	59,300	11,000	8,054	11,000	9,666
59,300	59,350	11,013	8,061	11,013	9,679
59,350	59,400	11,025	8,069	11,025	9,691
59,400	59,450	11,038	8,076	11,038	9,704
59,450	59,500	11,050	8,084	11,050	9,716
59,500	59,550	11,063	8,091	11,063	9,729
59,550	59,600	11,075	8,099	11,075	9,741
59,600	59,650	11,088	8,106	11,088	9,754
59,650	59,700	11,100	8,114	11,100	9,766
59,700	59,750	11,113	8,121	11,113	9,779
59,750	59,800	11,125	8,129	11,125	9,791
59,800	59,850	11,138	8,136	11,138	9,804
59,850	59,900	11,150	8,144	11,150	9,816
59,900	59,950	11,163	8,151	11,163	9,829
59,950	60,000	11,175	8,159	11,175	9,841
60,000					
60,000	60,050	11,188	8,166	11,188	9,854
60,050	60,100	11,200	8,174	11,200	9,866
60,100	60,150	11,213	8,181	11,213	9,879
60,150	60,200	11,225	8,189	11,225	9,891
60,200	60,250	11,238	8,196	11,238	9,904
60,250	60,300	11,250	8,204	11,250	9,916
60,300	60,350	11,263	8,211	11,263	9,929
60,350	60,400	11,275	8,219	11,275	9,941
60,400	60,450	11,288	8,226	11,288	9,954
60,450	60,500	11,300	8,234	11,300	9,966
60,500	60,550	11,313	8,241	11,313	9,979
60,550	60,600	11,325	8,249	11,325	9,991
60,600	60,650	11,338	8,256	11,338	10,004
60,650	60,700	11,350	8,264	11,350	10,016
60,700	60,750	11,363	8,271	11,363	10,029
60,750	60,800	11,375	8,279	11,375	10,041
60,800	60,850	11,388	8,286	11,388	10,054
60,850	60,900	11,400	8,294	11,400	10,066
60,900	60,950	11,413	8,301	11,413	10,079
60,950	61,000	11,425	8,309	11,425	10,091
61,000					
61,000	61,050	11,438	8,316	11,438	10,104
61,050	61,100	11,450	8,324	11,450	10,116
61,100	61,150	11,463	8,331	11,463	10,129
61,150	61,200	11,475	8,339	11,475	10,141
61,200	61,250	11,488	8,346	11,488	10,154
61,250	61,300	11,500	8,354	11,500	10,166
61,300	61,350	11,513	8,361	11,513	10,179
61,350	61,400	11,525	8,369	11,525	10,191
61,400	61,450	11,538	8,376	11,538	10,204
61,450	61,500	11,550	8,384	11,550	10,216
61,500	61,550	11,563	8,391	11,563	10,229
61,550	61,600	11,575	8,399	11,575	10,241
61,600	61,650	11,588	8,406	11,588	10,254
61,650	61,700	11,600	8,414	11,600	10,266
61,700	61,750	11,613	8,421	11,613	10,279
61,750	61,800	11,625	8,429	11,625	10,291
61,800	61,850	11,638	8,436	11,638	10,304
61,850	61,900	11,650	8,444	11,650	10,316
61,900	61,950	11,663	8,451	11,663	10,329
61,950	62,000	11,675	8,459	11,675	10,341
62,000					
62,000	62,050	11,688	8,466	11,688	10,354
62,050	62,100	11,700	8,474	11,700	10,366
62,100	62,150	11,713	8,481	11,713	10,379
62,150	62,200	11,725	8,489	11,725	10,391
62,200	62,250	11,738	8,496	11,738	10,404
62,250	62,300	11,750	8,504	11,750	10,416
62,300	62,350	11,763	8,511	11,763	10,429
62,350	62,400	11,775	8,519	11,775	10,441
62,400	62,450	11,788	8,526	11,788	10,454
62,450	62,500	11,800	8,534	11,800	10,466
62,500	62,550	11,813	8,541	11,813	10,479
62,550	62,600	11,825	8,549	11,825	10,491
62,600	62,650	11,838	8,556	11,838	10,504
62,650	62,700	11,850	8,564	11,850	10,516
62,700	62,750	11,863	8,571	11,863	10,529
62,750	62,800	11,875	8,579	11,875	10,541
62,800	62,850	11,888	8,586	11,888	10,554
62,850	62,900	11,900	8,594	11,900	10,566
62,900	62,950	11,913	8,601	11,913	10,579
62,950	63,000	11,925	8,609	11,925	10,591
63,000					
63,000	63,050	11,938	8,616	11,938	10,604
63,050	63,100	11,950	8,624	11,950	10,616
63,100	63,150	11,963	8,631	11,963	10,629
63,150	63,200	11,975	8,639	11,975	10,641
63,200	63,250	11,988	8,646	11,988	10,654
63,250	63,300	12,000	8,654	12,000	10,666
63,300	63,350	12,013	8,661	12,013	10,679
63,350	63,400	12,025	8,669	12,025	10,691
63,400	63,450	12,038	8,676	12,038	10,704
63,450	63,500	12,050	8,684	12,050	10,716
63,500	63,550	12,063	8,691	12,063	10,729
63,550	63,600	12,075	8,699	12,075	10,741
63,600	63,650	12,088	8,706	12,088	10,754
63,650	63,700	12,100	8,714	12,100	10,766
63,700	63,750	12,113	8,721	12,113	10,779
63,750	63,800	12,125	8,729	12,125	10,791
63,800	63,850	12,138	8,736	12,138	10,804
63,850	63,900	12,150	8,744	12,150	10,816
63,900	63,950	12,163	8,751	12,163	10,829
63,950	64,000	12,175	8,759	12,175	10,841
64,000					
64,000	64,050	12,188	8,766	12,188	10,854
64,050	64,100	12,200	8,774	12,200	10,866
64,100	64,150	12,213	8,781	12,213	10,879
64,150	64,200	12,225	8,789	12,225	10,891
64,200	64,250	12,238	8,796	12,238	10,904
64,250	64,300	12,250	8,804	12,250	10,916
64,300	64,350	12,263	8,811	12,263	10,929
64,350	64,400	12,275	8,819	12,275	10,941
64,400	64,450	12,288	8,826	12,288	10,954
64,450	64,500	12,300	8,834	12,300	10,966
64,500	64,550	12,313	8,841	12,313	10,979
64,550	64,600	12,325	8,849	12,325	10,991
64,600	64,650	12,338	8,856	12,338	11,004
64,650	64,700	12,350	8,864	12,350	11,016
64,700	64,750	12,363	8,871	12,363	11,029
64,750	64,800	12,375	8,879	12,375	11,041
64,800	64,850	12,388	8,886	12,388	11,054
64,850	64,900	12,400	8,894	12,400	11,066
64,900	64,950	12,413	8,901	12,413	11,079
64,950	65,000	12,425	8,909	12,425	11,091
65,000					
65,000	65,050	12,438	8,916	12,438	11,104
65,050	65,100	12,450	8,924	12,450	11,116
65,100	65,150	12,463	8,931	12,463	11,129
65,150	65,200	12,475	8,939	12,475	11,141
65,200	65,250	12,488	8,946	12,488	11,154
65,250	65,300	12,500	8,954	12,500	11,166
65,300	65,350	12,513	8,961	12,513	11,179
65,350	65,400	12,525	8,969	12,525	11,191
65,400	65,450	12,538	8,976	12,538	11,204
65,450	65,500	12,550	8,984	12,550	11,216
65,500	65,550	12,563	8,991	12,563	11,229
65,550	65,600	12,575	8,999	12,575	11,241
65,600	65,650	12,588	9,006	12,588	11,254
65,650	65,700	12,600	9,014	12,600	11,266
65,700	65,750	12,613	9,021	12,613	11,279
65,750	65,800	12,625	9,029	12,625	11,291
65,800	65,850	12,638	9,036	12,638	11,304
65,850	65,900	12,650	9,044	12,650	11,316
65,900	65,950	12,663	9,051	12,663	11,329
65,950	66,000	12,675	9,059	12,675	11,341
66,000					
66,000	66,050	12,688	9,066	12,688	11,354
66,050	66,100	12,700	9,074	12,700	11,366
66,100	66,150	12,713	9,081	12,713	11,379
66,150	66,200	12,725	9,089	12,725	11,391
66,200	66,250	12,738	9,096	12,738	11,404
66,250	66,300	12,750	9,104	12,750	11,416
66,300	66,350	12,763	9,111	12,763	11,429
66,350	66,400	12,775	9,119	12,775	11,441
66,400	66,450	12,788	9,126	12,788	11,454
66,450	66,500	12,800	9,134	12,800	11,466
66,500	66,550	12,813	9,141	12,813	11,479
66,550	66,600	12,825	9,149	12,825	11,491
66,600	66,650	12,838	9,156	12,838	11,504
66,650	66,700	12,850	9,164	12,850	11,516
66,700	66,750	12,863	9,171	12,863	11,529
66,750	66,800	12,875	9,179	12,875	11,541
66,800	66,850	12,888	9,186	12,888	11,554
66,850	66,900	12,900	9,194	12,900	11,566
66,900	66,950	12,913	9,201	12,913	11,579
66,950	67,000	12,925	9,209	12,925	11,591
67,000					
67,000	67,050	12,938	9,216	12,938	11,604
67,050	67,100	12,950	9,224	12,950	11,616
67,100	67,150	12,963	9,231	12,963	11,629
67,150	67,200	12,975	9,239	12,975	11,641
67,200	67,250	12,988	9,246	12,988	11,654
67,250	67,300	13,000	9,254	13,000	11,666
67,300	67,350	13,013	9,261	13,013	11,679
67,350	67,400	13,025	9,269	13,025	11,691
67,400	67,450	13,038	9,276	13,038	11,704
67,450	67,500	13,050	9,284	13,050	11,716
67,500	67,550	13,063	9,291	13,063	11,729
67,550	67,600	13,075	9,299	13,075	11,741
67,600	67,650	13,088	9,306	13,088	11,754
67,650	67,700	13,100	9,314	13,100	11,766
67,700	67,750	13,113	9,321	13,113	11,779
67,750	67,800	13,125	9,329	13,125	11,791
67,800	67,850	13,138	9,336	13,138	11,804
67,850	67,900	13,150	9,344	13,150	11,816
67,900	67,950	13,163	9,351	13,163	11,829
67,950	68,000	13,175	9,359	13,175	11,841

* This column must also be used by a qualifying widow(er).

(Continued on next page)

The Mathematics of Housing and Taxes, SV 9780547625645

Tax Table

If line 43 (taxable income) is—		And you are—			
At least	But less than	Single	Married filing jointly *	Married filing separately	Head of a household
		Your tax is—			

68,000

At least	But less than	Single	Married filing jointly	Married filing separately	Head of a household
68,000	68,050	13,188	9,369	13,188	11,854
68,050	68,100	13,200	9,381	13,200	11,866
68,100	68,150	13,213	9,394	13,213	11,879
68,150	68,200	13,225	9,406	13,225	11,891
68,200	68,250	13,238	9,419	13,238	11,904
68,250	68,300	13,250	9,431	13,250	11,916
68,300	68,350	13,263	9,444	13,263	11,929
68,350	68,400	13,275	9,456	13,275	11,941
68,400	68,450	13,288	9,469	13,288	11,954
68,450	68,500	13,300	9,481	13,300	11,966
68,500	68,550	13,313	9,494	13,313	11,979
68,550	68,600	13,325	9,506	13,325	11,991
68,600	68,650	13,338	9,519	13,338	12,004
68,650	68,700	13,350	9,531	13,351	12,016
68,700	68,750	13,363	9,544	13,365	12,029
68,750	68,800	13,375	9,556	13,379	12,041
68,800	68,850	13,388	9,569	13,393	12,054
68,850	68,900	13,400	9,581	13,407	12,066
68,900	68,950	13,413	9,594	13,421	12,079
68,950	69,000	13,425	9,606	13,435	12,091

69,000

At least	But less than	Single	Married filing jointly	Married filing separately	Head of a household
69,000	69,050	13,438	9,619	13,449	12,104
69,050	69,100	13,450	9,631	13,463	12,116
69,100	69,150	13,463	9,644	13,477	12,129
69,150	69,200	13,475	9,656	13,491	12,141
69,200	69,250	13,488	9,669	13,505	12,154
69,250	69,300	13,500	9,681	13,519	12,166
69,300	69,350	13,513	9,694	13,533	12,179
69,350	69,400	13,525	9,706	13,547	12,191
69,400	69,450	13,538	9,719	13,561	12,204
69,450	69,500	13,550	9,731	13,575	12,216
69,500	69,550	13,563	9,744	13,589	12,229
69,550	69,600	13,575	9,756	13,603	12,241
69,600	69,650	13,588	9,769	13,617	12,254
69,650	69,700	13,600	9,781	13,631	12,266
69,700	69,750	13,613	9,794	13,645	12,279
69,750	69,800	13,625	9,806	13,659	12,291
69,800	69,850	13,638	9,819	13,673	12,304
69,850	69,900	13,650	9,831	13,687	12,316
69,900	69,950	13,663	9,844	13,701	12,329
69,950	70,000	13,675	9,856	13,715	12,341

70,000

At least	But less than	Single	Married filing jointly	Married filing separately	Head of a household
70,000	70,050	13,688	9,869	13,729	12,354
70,050	70,100	13,700	9,881	13,743	12,366
70,100	70,150	13,713	9,894	13,757	12,379
70,150	70,200	13,725	9,906	13,771	12,391
70,200	70,250	13,738	9,919	13,785	12,404
70,250	70,300	13,750	9,931	13,799	12,416
70,300	70,350	13,763	9,944	13,813	12,429
70,350	70,400	13,775	9,956	13,827	12,441
70,400	70,450	13,788	9,969	13,841	12,454
70,450	70,500	13,800	9,981	13,855	12,466
70,500	70,550	13,813	9,994	13,869	12,479
70,550	70,600	13,825	10,006	13,883	12,491
70,600	70,650	13,838	10,019	13,897	12,504
70,650	70,700	13,850	10,031	13,911	12,516
70,700	70,750	13,863	10,044	13,925	12,529
70,750	70,800	13,875	10,056	13,939	12,541
70,800	70,850	13,888	10,069	13,953	12,554
70,850	70,900	13,900	10,081	13,967	12,566
70,900	70,950	13,913	10,094	13,981	12,579
70,950	71,000	13,925	10,106	13,995	12,591

71,000

At least	But less than	Single	Married filing jointly	Married filing separately	Head of a household
71,000	71,050	13,938	10,119	14,009	12,604
71,050	71,100	13,950	10,131	14,023	12,616
71,100	71,150	13,963	10,144	14,037	12,629
71,150	71,200	13,975	10,156	14,051	12,641
71,200	71,250	13,988	10,169	14,065	12,654
71,250	71,300	14,000	10,181	14,079	12,666
71,300	71,350	14,013	10,194	14,093	12,679
71,350	71,400	14,025	10,206	14,107	12,691
71,400	71,450	14,038	10,219	14,121	12,704
71,450	71,500	14,050	10,231	14,135	12,716
71,500	71,550	14,063	10,244	14,149	12,729
71,550	71,600	14,075	10,256	14,163	12,741
71,600	71,650	14,088	10,269	14,177	12,754
71,650	71,700	14,100	10,281	14,191	12,766
71,700	71,750	14,113	10,294	14,205	12,779
71,750	71,800	14,125	10,306	14,219	12,791
71,800	71,850	14,138	10,319	14,233	12,804
71,850	71,900	14,150	10,331	14,247	12,816
71,900	71,950	14,163	10,344	14,261	12,829
71,950	72,000	14,175	10,356	14,275	12,841

72,000

At least	But less than	Single	Married filing jointly	Married filing separately	Head of a household
72,000	72,050	14,188	10,369	14,289	12,854
72,050	72,100	14,200	10,381	14,303	12,866
72,100	72,150	14,213	10,394	14,317	12,879
72,150	72,200	14,225	10,406	14,331	12,891
72,200	72,250	14,238	10,419	14,345	12,904
72,250	72,300	14,250	10,431	14,359	12,916
72,300	72,350	14,263	10,444	14,373	12,929
72,350	72,400	14,275	10,456	14,387	12,941
72,400	72,450	14,288	10,469	14,401	12,954
72,450	72,500	14,300	10,481	14,415	12,966
72,500	72,550	14,313	10,494	14,429	12,979
72,550	72,600	14,325	10,506	14,443	12,991
72,600	72,650	14,338	10,519	14,457	13,004
72,650	72,700	14,350	10,531	14,471	13,016
72,700	72,750	14,363	10,544	14,485	13,029
72,750	72,800	14,375	10,556	14,499	13,041
72,800	72,850	14,388	10,569	14,513	13,054
72,850	72,900	14,400	10,581	14,527	13,066
72,900	72,950	14,413	10,594	14,541	13,079
72,950	73,000	14,425	10,606	14,555	13,091

73,000

At least	But less than	Single	Married filing jointly	Married filing separately	Head of a household
73,000	73,050	14,438	10,619	14,569	13,104
73,050	73,100	14,450	10,631	14,583	13,116
73,100	73,150	14,463	10,644	14,597	13,129
73,150	73,200	14,475	10,656	14,611	13,141
73,200	73,250	14,488	10,669	14,625	13,154
73,250	73,300	14,500	10,681	14,639	13,166
73,300	73,350	14,513	10,694	14,653	13,179
73,350	73,400	14,525	10,706	14,667	13,191
73,400	73,450	14,538	10,719	14,681	13,204
73,450	73,500	14,550	10,731	14,695	13,216
73,500	73,550	14,563	10,744	14,709	13,229
73,550	73,600	14,575	10,756	14,723	13,241
73,600	73,650	14,588	10,769	14,737	13,254
73,650	73,700	14,600	10,781	14,751	13,266
73,700	73,750	14,613	10,794	14,765	13,279
73,750	73,800	14,625	10,806	14,779	13,291
73,800	73,850	14,638	10,819	14,793	13,304
73,850	73,900	14,650	10,831	14,807	13,316
73,900	73,950	14,663	10,844	14,821	13,329
73,950	74,000	14,675	10,856	14,835	13,341

74,000

At least	But less than	Single	Married filing jointly	Married filing separately	Head of a household
74,000	74,050	14,688	10,869	14,849	13,354
74,050	74,100	14,700	10,881	14,863	13,366
74,100	74,150	14,713	10,894	14,877	13,379
74,150	74,200	14,725	10,906	14,891	13,391
74,200	74,250	14,738	10,919	14,905	13,404
74,250	74,300	14,750	10,931	14,919	13,416
74,300	74,350	14,763	10,944	14,933	13,429
74,350	74,400	14,775	10,956	14,947	13,441
74,400	74,450	14,788	10,969	14,961	13,454
74,450	74,500	14,800	10,981	14,975	13,466
74,500	74,550	14,813	10,994	14,989	13,479
74,550	74,600	14,825	11,006	15,003	13,491
74,600	74,650	14,838	11,019	15,017	13,504
74,650	74,700	14,850	11,031	15,031	13,516
74,700	74,750	14,863	11,044	15,045	13,529
74,750	74,800	14,875	11,056	15,059	13,541
74,800	74,850	14,888	11,069	15,073	13,554
74,850	74,900	14,900	11,081	15,087	13,566
74,900	74,950	14,913	11,094	15,101	13,579
74,950	75,000	14,925	11,106	15,115	13,591

75,000

At least	But less than	Single	Married filing jointly	Married filing separately	Head of a household
75,000	75,050	14,938	11,119	15,129	13,604
75,050	75,100	14,950	11,131	15,143	13,616
75,100	75,150	14,963	11,144	15,157	13,629
75,150	75,200	14,975	11,156	15,171	13,641
75,200	75,250	14,988	11,169	15,185	13,654
75,250	75,300	15,000	11,181	15,199	13,666
75,300	75,350	15,013	11,194	15,213	13,679
75,350	75,400	15,025	11,206	15,227	13,691
75,400	75,450	15,038	11,219	15,241	13,704
75,450	75,500	15,050	11,231	15,255	13,716
75,500	75,550	15,063	11,244	15,269	13,729
75,550	75,600	15,075	11,256	15,283	13,741
75,600	75,650	15,088	11,269	15,297	13,754
75,650	75,700	15,100	11,281	15,311	13,766
75,700	75,750	15,113	11,294	15,325	13,779
75,750	75,800	15,125	11,306	15,339	13,791
75,800	75,850	15,138	11,319	15,353	13,804
75,850	75,900	15,150	11,331	15,367	13,816
75,900	75,950	15,163	11,344	15,381	13,829
75,950	76,000	15,175	11,356	15,395	13,841

76,000

At least	But less than	Single	Married filing jointly	Married filing separately	Head of a household
76,000	76,050	15,188	11,369	15,409	13,854
76,050	76,100	15,200	11,381	15,423	13,866
76,100	76,150	15,213	11,394	15,437	13,879
76,150	76,200	15,225	11,406	15,451	13,891
76,200	76,250	15,238	11,419	15,465	13,904
76,250	76,300	15,250	11,431	15,479	13,916
76,300	76,350	15,263	11,444	15,493	13,929
76,350	76,400	15,275	11,456	15,507	13,941
76,400	76,450	15,288	11,469	15,521	13,954
76,450	76,500	15,300	11,481	15,535	13,966
76,500	76,550	15,313	11,494	15,549	13,979
76,550	76,600	15,325	11,506	15,563	13,991
76,600	76,650	15,338	11,519	15,577	14,004
76,650	76,700	15,350	11,531	15,591	14,016
76,700	76,750	15,363	11,544	15,605	14,029
76,750	76,800	15,375	11,556	15,619	14,041
76,800	76,850	15,388	11,569	15,633	14,054
76,850	76,900	15,400	11,581	15,647	14,066
76,900	76,950	15,413	11,594	15,661	14,079
76,950	77,000	15,425	11,606	15,675	14,091

* This column must also be used by a qualifying widow(er).

Support Materials:
Glossary

Glossary

adjustable rate mortgage (A.R.M.) A mortgage on which the interest rate may go up or down as interest rates in general fluctuate.

annual percentage rate (APR) A calculation, developed as part of the Truth in Lending Act, that tries to reflect the costs to borrow.

appreciation An increase in value as general market values go up. In housing, this may be because of inflation, greater demand, rising building costs, population increase, or scarcity of vacant land.

area The number of square units needed to cover the surface bounded by a 2-dimensional figure such as a rectangle or a circle.

assessed valuation The value of a property, as officially determined by a local government for taxation purposes. Assessed Valuation = Assessment Rate × Market Value

closing costs Fees related to buying a house or condominium, and paid by the buyer before moving in. Closing costs vary, but may include lawyer's services, title search, and inspection of the property. Bank service charges, referred to as **points**, may be included. Each point is 1% of the mortgage amount.

compatible numbers Numbers used to estimate answers in division. They are close in value to the given divisor and dividend, and divide evenly.

compound interest Interest calculated by periodically (quarterly, or even daily) adding earned interest to an account. The principal then increases or decreases more rapidly than with simple interest.

condominium An apartment that is owned, rather than rented. Each owner pays a monthly **maintenance fee** for the care of the building and grounds.

condominium association dues Also "condo dues." (See **maintenance fees**.)

contractor A person or company who agrees to provide materials and perform work, usually for a certain price and in a given length of time.

depreciation A decrease in value as general market values go down. In housing, this may be because of challenges in the economy as a whole. Also known as **negative appreciation** among real estate agents and mortgage professionals.

down payment A portion of the purchase price paid by the customer at time of purchase, to reduce monthly loan payments and to encourage lenders to lend.

Federal withholding tax   A percentage of an employee's taxable pay, deducted and paid directly by the employer to the Internal Revenue Service of the Federal government. State and city income taxes are collected in a similar way.

fixed rate mortgage   A mortgage on which the interest rate remains the same throughout the term of the mortgage.

gross pay   A worker's full pay, before taxes or any other amounts are taken out.

home equity loan   Money borrowed on the owner's invested value in a house, which serves as security. As is the case with any mortgage, the lender gets the right to take over the house if the loan is not repaid.

homeowner's association dues   Also "HOA dues." (See **maintenance fees**.)

homeowner's insurance   A contract by which a person pays a **premium** to an insurance company. In return, the company agrees to pay money, as specified in a written policy, to cover loss or damage to the property (by fire, for example). Such insurance usually excludes causes of loss such as flood, earthquake, and nuclear accident. Most owners insure a property for its full **replacement value**, which would cover reconstruction if it were destroyed.

income tax   (See **Federal withholding tax**.)

insurance   (See **homeowner's insurance**.)

interest rate   (See **compound interest**; **simple interest**.)

kilowatt-hour   A unit of energy, equivalent to 1,000 watts of electricity used for 1 hour.

loan   Money lent at interest. The interest depends upon the amount borrowed, the interest rate (**Annual Percentage Rate**), and the time it takes to repay the loan.

maintenance fee   Associated with **condominiums**, this is normally a monthly fee that all residents pay against necessary maintenance and repairs to common areas.

map scale   A rate (ratio) between two sets of measurements. It tells how many miles are represented by a unit (usually an inch) on a map.

market value   An approximation of the amount a property could be sold for.

mean   (average) A single number used to represent a set of numbers; found by dividing the sum of the numbers by the number of numbers.

median   The middle value when a set of numbers are listed in order.

mode   The number that occurs most often in a set of numbers.

mortgage   Money borrowed to buy a house or a condominium. The amount is approximately the purchase price less the **down payment**. The mortgage is repaid in periodic payments that include interest, and sometimes taxes.

move-in costs   Costs, in addition to rent, that must be paid when a renter moves into a residence. These may include a **rental agent fee** and/or a **security deposit** to the landlord. Sometimes, utility deposits are also required.

net pay   (What is left of) a worker's pay after taxes and other regular deductions—e.g., for health care premiums—are subtracted out.

payroll deductions   Money subtracted from a worker's full (**gross**) pay. The deductions cover taxes, insurance, and sometimes special amounts such as contributions or investments. The amount the worker receives, after deductions, is called the **net**—or "take-home"—**pay**.

percent   A ratio that compares a number to 100. 10 percent (10%) means 10 hundredths, or 10 per 100.

perimeter   The distance around the outer boundary of a 2-dimensional figure such as a rectangle or a square.

premium   In insurance, money paid by the policyholder for coverage under a contract (policy).

P&I, PIT, PITI, PITIMI   Shorthand for "Principal, Interest, Taxes, Insurance, and Mortgage Insurance," this is a means of referring to the components of the monthly mortgage payment. (Note: Homeowner Association Dues are not included in this acronym, though lenders consider them part of the payment when they are deciding whether to approve a request for mortgage financing.)

principal balance   In the case of a mortgage or other loan, this is the amount owed, not counting any interest that is due, at any given time during the life of the loan.

real estate taxes   Money collected by local governments and used to pay for municipal services and schools. The real estate tax is based on the **assessed valuation** of a property, which is a percent of the property's **market value**.

remodeling   Rebuilding all or part of a structure.

rental agent fee   Sometimes agents charge a fee to help you find an apartment.

replacement value   In insurance, simply the amount that they estimate it will cost to replace the insured property.

rounding   Replacing a number with an approximation to a nearest given unit, such as to the nearest hundred or tenth. Also, a mixed number can be rounded to the nearest whole number.

scale drawing   A diagram, with dimensions that are in a fixed ratio to the object it represents. A scale drawing may be a reduction (as the blueprints of a house) or an enlargement (as a diagram of a small insect).

secured/unsecured loans   A secured loan is money lent with the understanding that if it is not repaid, some property (house, automobile, furniture) can be taken by the person who made the loan. The property is usually whatever has been bought with the borrowed money.
An unsecured loan has the guarantee of the borrower's word that the money will be repaid, but there is no property held as security.

security deposit   Money (usually one or two month's rent) collected and held during the period a renter occupies a residence. All or part of the deposit can be retained by the landlord if the dwelling is damaged by the renter.

simple interest   A payment for the use of money. The amount of interest depends on the **interest rate** (expressed as an annual percent), on the **principal balance** (the amount of money in the account—or the amount of the mortgage, in the case of various **home equity loans**, for instance), and on the length of time (in years) that the money is used—also referred to as the **term**, in the case of loans.

Social Security   The Federal Insurance Contributions Act; an insurance and pension plan contributed to, in equal shares, by employees and employers. The plan covers the cost of medical, retirement, and disability benefits paid to employees who have contributed, or to their families.

term   For mortgages and home equity loans, the total number of months that the borrower agrees to pay down the loan—i.e., the "life of the loan."

utilities   Goods and services such as electricity, natural gas, water, oil, and telephone.

withholding tax   (See **Federal withholding tax**.)

Support Materials:
Answer Key

Answer Key

Part I: Math Skills and Concepts
Pages 8-9
Pre-Skills Test

1. 7; 17
2. 5; 19
3. 2; 12
4. 4; 14
5. 8; 18
6. 6; 16
7. 7; 6
8. 3; 13
9. 8
10. 15
11. 6
12. 12
13. 7
14. 14
15. 9
16. 5
17. 3
18. 8
19. 8
20. 4
21. 9
22. 7
23. 5
24. 40
25. 15
26. 16
27. 12
28. 45
29. 49
30. 56
31. 3
32. 6
33. 8
34. 8
35. 7
36. 8
37. 9
38. 7
39. 10
40. 16
41. 20
42. 21
43. 4
44. 36
45. $\frac{4}{13}$
46. $\frac{6}{13}$
47. $\frac{3}{13}$
48. $\frac{10}{13}$
49. 6%
50. 16%
51. 80%
52. 49%
53. 21%
54. 93%

Pages 12-13
Practice

1. 32.13
2. 1,202
3. 28.47
4. 877
5. 35.22
6. 52.91
7. 3,045
8. 8.64
9. 28.28
10. 18 R1
11. 0.9
12. 0.104
13. 8,497
14. 2,903
15. 32.65
16. 512
17. 28.78
18. 20.29
19. 663
20. 5.2
21. 0.36
22. 20 R3
23. 754 R4
24. 3.08 R2
25. 2.5
26. 0.7
27. 2.15
28. 0.98
29. 3,285 miles
30. $44.45
31. 385 miles
32. $1.08
33. 2,653 miles
34. $126
35. $1.20
36. 438 miles

Pages 16-17
Practice

1. 23%
2. 7%
3. 186%
4. 63%
5. 5.8%
6. 900%
7. 0.25; 25%
8. 0.875; 87.5%
9. 0.4; 40%
10. 3.5; 350%
11. 9.125; 912.5%
12. 5.6; 560%
13. 0.24
14. 0.18
15. 0.02
16. 0.028
17. 0.0005
18. 4.38
19. $\frac{7}{10}$
20. $\frac{2}{5}$
21. $\frac{17}{20}$
22. $1\frac{1}{10}$
23. $1\frac{87}{100}$
24. $2\frac{1}{25}$
25. 4
26. 6
27. 40
28. 6
29. 42
30. 12
31. 63
32. 36.5
33. 6
34. 24
35. 1.9
36. 13
37. 36 miles
38. 22
39. 28 minutes
40. $122.40
41. $525
42. a. 12
   b. 18

Page 19
Practice

1. 25
2. 15
3. 30
4. 55
5. See student chart.

Page 21
Practice

1. 90
2. 5.1
3. 357
4. 68
5. 14
6. 0.37
7. 13
8. 12
9. 5.6
10. 4.4
11. 3
12. 1.8
13. 75.3; 78; none
14. 6.3; 6.3; none
15. 237.5; 220; 220
16. 83.2; 84; 75
17. 6.6; 5.9; 5.9
18. 7.5; 7.5; 7.5

Extension

1. 23
2. 69, 68
3. 69
4. a. 483
   b. 476
   c. 134
5. 69.09

Support Materials
The Mathematics of Housing and Taxes, SV 9780547625645

Page 23
Think About It
1. Addition and multiplication, they are commutative
2. one of the calculators applies order of operations automatically

Practice
1. 1,148,405
2. 7,235
3. 575
4. 698.83
5. 7,326.88
6. 135.31
7. 1900
8. 0.07
9. 18.3
10. 116.5
11. 0.13
12. 0.06
13. 901.287
14. 4.536
15. 5,249 miles
16. 0.0084 cm thick

Page 25
Think About It
1. Answers may vary.

Practice
1. 63
2. 63
3. 617
4. 65¢
5. $9.71
6. 8.36
7. 54
8. 145
9. 6¢
10. $395
11. $0.39
12. 1.65
13. 530
14. 5.32
15. 57,850
16. 1.83
17. 0.255
18. 20.66
19. $591
20. $78.50

Extension
1. 3,100
2. 5,500
3. 5,500

Page 27
Think About It
1. Answers may vary.
2. Answers may vary.

Practice
1. 500
2. 1,250
3. $9
4. $6
5. 850
6. 1.1
7. 38,000
8. 0.033
9. 270
10. 50,000
11. $0.80
12. $17
13. 170
14. 4.2
15. $716
16. $3
17. $100

Page 29
Think About It
1. Answers may vary.

Practice
1. 250,000
2. $500
3. $700
4. 350
5. 27
6. 210
7. $280
8. 180
9. 0.18
10. 5
11. 4.5
12. 3
13. 2
14. 7
15. 50
16. 18
17. 6
18. 50
19. $3
20. 4
21. $120
22. 4

Page 31
Think About It
1. Answers may vary.
2. Answers may vary.

Practice
1. mental computation
2. paper and pencil or calculator
3. calculator
4. calculator
5. calculator, or pencil and paper (130 miles)
6. calculator, or pencil and paper ($28.57)

Pages 32-33
Part I Review
1. b
2. b
3. b
4. 9,937
5. 31
6. 3,495
7. 52,977
8. 10.54
9. 2.66
10. 96
11. 1,971
12. 21.18
13. 576
14. 214
15. 0.1
16. 5%
17. 300%
18. 365%
19. 62%
20. 8%
21. 2.5%
22. 0.29
23. 0.025
24. 4
25. 20
26. 12
27. 140
28. 12,334
29. 1,945.2894
30. 28.942
31. 19.9884
32. 649
33. 93
34. 5.22
35. 65.778
36. 10,000
37. 11
38. 0.04
39. 35
40. 35
41. 7
42. 2,259
43. 1,070
44. about 20 in.
45. no

Pages 34-35
Part I Test
1. 947
2. 52.17
3. 3,170
4. 33
5. 3,592
6. 2.42
7. 234
8. 2,456
9. 73.8
10. 754 R4
11. 1.4
12. 3.085
13. 3.09
14. 1.39
15. 0.87
16. 61%
17. 4.6%
18. 60%
19. 125%
20. 200.1%
21. 20%
22. 0.025; $\frac{1}{40}$
23. 0.5; $\frac{50}{100} = \frac{1}{2}$

24. 1.5; $1\frac{1}{2}$ **25.** 13.2

26. 13   **27.** 13

28. 10,009   **29.** 19.74

30. 2,353   **31.** 37.65

32. 86.2   **33.** 5.8426

34. 703   **35.** $405

36. 15.34   **37.** 16

38. $2.42   **39.** 4,100

40. 5.89   **41.** 11.3

42. 2.906   **43.** 1,700

44. 200   **45.** $11

46. 2   **47.** 4,900

48. 7   **49.** b

50. c   **51.** $14.75

52. 2 packs of cards

53. 14

Part II: Taxes
Pages 37-38
Pre-Skills Test

1. $1,833.18

2. $1,354

3. $7,337.09

4. $2,177.21

5. $1,220.75

6. $32,489.69

7. $761

8. $1,022

9. $186.04

10. $1,035.22

11. $344.36

12. $1,719.63

13. 0.02

14. 0.05

15. 0.035

16. 0.065

17. 0.075

18. 0.0275

19. $100

20. $150

21. $525

22. $24.32

23. $293.82

24. $1,013.68

25. $170

26. $536.25

27. $2,157.18

28. At least $23,850, but less than $23,900

29. At least $23,800 but less than $23,850

30. At least $31,900 but less than $31,950

31. At least $31,000 but less than $31,050

32. At least $31,450 but less than $31,500

33. At least $23,600 but less than $23,650

34. At least $23,250 but less than $23,300

35. At least $31,050 but less than $31,100

Pages 40-42
Think About It

1. Answers may vary.

2. Answers may vary.

Practice

1. $4,835.35

2. $2,128.83

3. 0

4. 0

5. $37,850

6. $49,260

7. $67,207

8. $70,945

9. $83,249

10. $25,710

11. $18,721

12. $32,926

13. $21,331

14. $83,331

15. $60,032

16. $35,763

17. $62,007

18. $27,878

19. $82,227

20. $38,222

21. $23,305.50

22. $29,344.09

23. $55,822.65

24. $44,701.09

25. $47,820.49

26. $21,972

27. $3,295.80

28. $1,648.90

29. $472.40

30. $164.79

31. $315.26

Pages 44-46
Think About It

1. They may have different filling statuses.

Practice

1. AGI = $39,376. TI = $30,026

2. AGI = $94,672. TI = $73,022

3. owe $296.65

4. refund $988.89

5. refund $425.13

6. owe $103.46

7. $1,208   **8.** $1,258

9 $1,273   **10.** $1,498

11. $1,520   **12.** $1,528

13. $1,356   **14.** $1,386

15. $1,439   **16.** $1,625

17. $1,640   **18.** $1,678

19. AGI = $24,624

Taxable income = $15,274

Tax (from chart) = $1,873

20. AGI = $79,330

Taxable income =

$65,605

Tax (from chart) = $12,588

21. AGI = $67,324

Taxable income = $57,459

Tax (from chart) = $10,550

22. AGI = $59,426

Taxable income = $45,376

Tax (from chart) = $5,969

23. AGI = $65,000

Taxable income = $54,175

Tax (from chart) = $9,725

24. AGI = $82,333

Taxable income = $54,836

Tax (from chart) = $8,554

25. AGI = $77,461

Taxable income = $63,255

Tax (from chart) = $8,654

26. AGI = $56,872

Taxable income = $39,772

Tax (from chart) = $5,369

Pages 48-50
Problem Solving
Application
1. $800
2. $923.75
3. $2,656.25
4. $3,612.05
5. $4,900
6. $11,806.25
7. $16,935.25
8. $20,807.65
9. $41,589.25
10. $58,904.75

11. $108,893.75
12. $135,479.75
13. $657.50
14. $0
15. $198.50
16. $6,956.25
17. $456.25
18. $0
19. $10,163.75
20. $1,774.25
21. $0
22. $24,068.53
23. $0
24. $931.47
25. $9,323.75
26. $13,581.75
27. a. $13,556.25
    b. $9,737.50
    c. $25.50 less
    d. $3,844.25 less
28. $100,541
29. $21,771.75
30. $11,875
31. $9,387.75
32. $13,378.75

Pages 53-54
Practice
1. $21,050.37
2. $21,292.05
3. $11,942.05
4. $1,581.31
5. $1,370
6. $211.31
7. Line 1: $23,125.35
8. Line 2: $109.08
9. Line 4: $23,234.43
10. Line 5: $9,350
11. Line 6: $13,884.43
12. Line 7: $3,558
13. Line 10: $3,558

14. Line 11: $1,663
15. Stacey received a refund.
16. $1,895

Pages 57-58
Think About It
1. Homeowners may have both mortgage interest and property taxes to deduct.
2. The IRS does not have to accept any deductions not supported by records.

Practice
1. $1,163   2. $75
3. $683   4. $51
5. $12,002   6. $6,302
7. Standard   8. Standard
9. Itemized   10. Itemized
11. itemized deduction; $9,095
12. itemized deduction; $18,156

Pages 60-62
Think About It
1. Examples: sales tax, real estate tax;
2. Because they were unable to raise enough through sales and real estate taxes.

Practice
1. $137.44   2. $355.34
3. $694.98   4. $643.10
5. $2,161.77   6. $332.34
7. $144.80   8. $644.15
9. $464.75   10. $1,209.19
11. $252.30   12. $1,659.19
13. $113.61   14. $127.02
15. $902.39   16. $225.17
17. $403.43   18. $976.76
19. $1,321.06
20. $740.72   21. $628.41

22. $69.72 (Refund)

23. $1,750.00 **24.** $17,718.12

25. $395.13

26. $23.19 (Refund)

27. $1,487.81

28. $273.40 (Owe)

29. $4,150.00

30. $28,662.41

31. $778.18

32. $68.97 (Owe)

Pages 64-66
Problem Solving Strategy Practice

1. $2.600   **2.** $1,600

3. $1,000   **4.** 2

5. $500   **6.** $5,550

7. $3,450   **8.** $2,100

9. 1   **10.** $2,100

11. $240   **12.** $175

13. $1,075   **14.** $1,300

15. $50

16. Federal: $1,912.50
State: $765
City: $148.75

17. $212.50   **18.** $45

19. $1,250   **20.** $800

21. $100

22. Federal: $2,100; State: $720; City: $180; Total: $3,000

Pages 68-70
Decision Making

1. $332

2. IRA: $275

3. $25,119

4. $3,650

5. $2,714

6. $5,700

7. Married, joint

8. $46,820

9. $435

10. $44,755

11. $7,300

12. $3,502

13. $11,400

14. Single

15. $25,735

16. 0

17. Form 1040EZ because a standard deduction will be taken.

18. Form 1040A because a standard deduction will be taken.

19. Form 1040EZ because a standard deduction will be taken, interest income is less than $400, there are no adjustments or dependents, and the person is single.

20. Yes. She will need to complete 1099-G.

21. No. Student loan deductions cannot be made using 1040EZ.

22. No. Miscellaneous income cannot be claimed using 1040EZ.

23. No. She made too much money.

24. Yes. He is within the parameters.

25. No, because he gets pension income, he must file 1040A or 1040.

26. She must file 1040 because she has gambling winnings.

Pages 71-72
Money Tips

1. To have more money available on a regular basis

2. Shortly after you file your taxes in April for the previous year

3. Neither. But other factors will affect the tax you owe.

4. Work with a tax accountant to determine the correct number of deductions.

5. The government is earning interest on that money instead of you.

6. Answers may vary.

7. e.g., invest to earn interest

8. Answers may vary.

Page 74
Calculator

1. 36   **2.** 37

3. 20   **4.** 31.3

5. 88.06   **6.** 497.5

7. 0.6   **8.** 42.1

9. 5.2   **10.** $6,150

11. $97

12. Answers will vary.

Pages 75-76
Part II Review

1. b

2. b

3. a

4. $23,462.18

5. 1,948.72

6. $305.18

7. $183.46

8. $1,794.86

9. $246.87

10. $23,709.05

11. $26,556

12. $15,556

13. $1,670

14. $3,650

15. Standard deduction

Support Materials
The Mathematics of Housing and Taxes, SV 9780547625645

16. $648.70

Page 77
Part II Test
1. $23,934.19;
2. $1,631.92
3. $339.03
4. $115.27
5. $1,797.46
6. AGI = $46,887 / TI = $41,187 / Fed. Tax = $6,475
7. AGI = $64,478 / TI = $53,078 / Fed. Tax = $7,124
8. Fed. Tax = $1000 / State Tax = $417.50 / City Tax = $105
9. $850

Part III: Housing
Pages 79-80
Pre-Skills Test
1. $43,770
2. $67,190
3. $203,410
4. $308,792
5. $22,320
6. $21,875
7. $35,728
8. $42,998
9. $216,000
10. $139,400
11. $652,572
12. $73,830
13. $36,306
14. $68,878.40
15. $1,200
16. $3,105
17. $3,192.75
18. $7,656.38
19. $150,000
20. $139,196.43

21. $210,625
22. $388,442.86
23. 5   24. 4
25. 4   26. 3
27. 8   28. 12
29. 9 ft   30. 12 ft
31. 42 ft   32. 108 sq ft
33. 12 sq yd

Pages 82-84
Think About It
1. Answers may vary.
2. Answers may vary.

Practice
1. $728   2. $1,050
3. $1,166.67   4. $548.51
5. $1,386.67: $388.27
6. $1,473.33: $412.53
7. $1,646.67: $461.07
8. $1,733.33: $485.33
9. $1,820: $509.60
10. $1,906.67: $533.87
11. $2,080: $582.40
12. $2,253.33: $630.93
13. $2,426.67: $679.47
14. $2,374.42: $664.84
15. $446   16. $471
17. $560   18. $709
19. $544   20. $501
21. $744
22. Hastings House
23. $1,058.75
24. $1,067
25. $1,650
26. $3,019.50
27. $3,290.25
28. $2,100
29. $650
30. $1,415
31. $1,213.24

Page 86
Problem Solving
Application
1. $355
2. $404
3. $49
4. Jefferson Manor includes covered parking.
5. No; she pays $9.00 less.
6. $2,370
7. $3,232
8. $5,505
9. Jefferson; three rooms
10. Jefferson Manor
11. Washington Rooming House

Pages 88-90
Practice
1. $82,000; $100,000
2. $73,000; $114,600
3. $81,640; $109,260
4. $143,000; $195,600
5. $90,240; $95,240
6. $169,800; $194,209
7. $2,500
8. $52,500
9. $72,265
10. $926
11. $93,526
12. $12,656.70
13. $153,286.70
14. $6,000
15. $206,000
16. 0%
17. $200,000
18. 2%
19. $212,160
20. $0

Think About It
1. Students should explain that a house appreciates

in value because of its location, its commuting distance to a city, its nearness to various attractions, and the state of the economy. Houses depreciate due to factors affecting the overall economy.

More Practice
1. $47,338.20
2. $193,385.36
3. $187,550
4. $199,517.76
5. $353,394.14
6. $99,497.44
7. $418,500
8. 15%
9. $525,706.25
10. $137,200

Extension
1. Ed's house
2. $17,675.49

Pages 93-94
Think About It
1. Condominiums tend to be less expensive, and their taxes tend to be less, as well.
2. Assessments of needed maintenance can unexpectedly add thousands of dollars to a condo-dweller's expenses.

Practice
1. $35,600, $1,253.76
2. $50,000, $1,623.64
3. $3,500, $798.56
4. $3,500
5. $4,464.29
6. $7,857.14
7. $9,928.57

8. $12,678.57
9. $14,285.71
10. $37,520; $1249.80
11. $35,000; $1,029.55
12. about $3,400

Extension
1. In 2 years, maintenance fees will be $210.
2. In 2 years, the monthly payment will be $1,444.47.

Pages 96-98
Think About It
1. The monthly payment per $1,000 for 11% ($9.53) is about $0.80 more than for 10% ($8.78). You can mentally multiply 50 × $0.80 to get $40 extra per month at 11%.

Practice
1. $1,326.75
2. $995.68
3. $1,575.20
4. $939.75
5. $876.66
6. $24,800
7. $99,200
8. $907.68
9. $8,970
10. $80,730
11. $779.85
12. $28,086
13. $65,534
14. $642.89
15. $11,976
16. $67,864
17. $570.74
18. $2,160
19. $1,720
20. $5,395
21. $3,361.25

22. $3,876.25
23. $37,800
24. $151,200
25. $858.82
26. $28,970
27. $260,730
28. $1,720.82
29. $117,900
30. $275,100
31. $1,771.64
32. $119,750
33. $359,250
34. $2,270.46

Extension
1. $778.65
2. $643.86
3. $1,267.20
4. $980.00
5. $693.12
6. $834.62
7. $1,627.08
8. $1,829.42
9. $2,040.54
10. $592

Pages 100-102
Think About It
1. Tax rate increases when costs increase, or when a locality loses property from its tax rolls.
2. Banks earn interest on the money they hold until taxes are paid.

Practice
1. $76,000
2. $88,500
3. $172,900
4. $129,285
5. $310,791
6. $2,391.96
7. $2,099.02
8. $1,975.68
9. $2,323.56
10. $5,242.56
11. $721
12. $824
13. $878
14. $780
15. $945
16. $87,500
17. $52,250
18. $87,750; $2,886.98
19. $71,920; $3,042.22
20. $804.58
21. $712.52

Extension

1. The new assessed valuation for a $100,000 house is $100,000. The annual tax on this house is $3,200. $3,200 ÷ $100,000 = 0.032, or $3.20 per $100.

Pages 104-106
Think About It

1. Renters don't have a mortgage and aren't required to carry insurance, so they may assume that the apartment complex has insurance covering the building.

2. Losses due to theft or fire can be costly to replace.

Practice

1. $7,800
2. $39,000
3. $15,600
4. $3,900
5. $10,950
6. $54,750
7. $21,900
8. $5,475
9. $8,764.50
10. $43,822
11. $17,529
12. $4,382.25
13. $2,500
14. $5,000
15. $5,000
16. $10,000
17. $7,500
18. $15,000

Extension

1. 234,360
2. 138,880
3. 34,720
4. 60,760
5. Answers may vary.
6. $12,200
7. $61,000
8. $24,400
9. $6,100
10. $19,280
11. $96,400
12. $38,560
13. $9,640
14. $10,720

---

15. $53,600
16. $21,440
17. $5,360
18. $8,285
19. $41,425
20. $16,570
21. $4,142.50
22. $26,124
23. $130,620
24. $52,248
25. $13,062

Pages 108-110
Think About It

1. Answers may vary.
2. Answers may vary.

Practice

1. 23,592 kWh
2. 13,587 kWh
3. 3,195 kWh
4. 2,873
5. $141.64
6. 1,201
7. $72.42
8. 17,637
9. $419.76
10. 7,581
11. $407.10
12. $82.89
13. $150.76
14. $30.60
15. $153.93
16. 3.051
17. $43.87
18. 2.134
19. $28.81
20. 4.892
21. $54.94
22. 4.809
23. $76.22

Extension

1. $1,073
2. $188.50
3. $145
4. $43.50

Page 112
Problem Solving Application

1. $84
2. $8.01
3. $306.60
4. $38.33
5. $124.80
6. $108
7. $1.24
8. Clothes dryer

Page 114
Problem Solving Application
Think About It

1. Answers may vary.
2. Winter

Practice

1. 486 gallons
2. 30 months
3. 48 months
4. 729 gallons
5. $178.20
6. $623.70

Pages 117-118
Think About It

1. For every 50 feet of perimeter, there is 400 square feet of wall. One gallon covers 400 square feet.
2. Answers may vary.

Practice

1. 58 ft
2. 42 ft
3. 56 ft
4. 60 ft
5. 2 gal; $27.90
6. 2 gal; $34.10
7. 3 gal; $31.95
8. $1,512
9. $2,016
10. $3,024
11. $l = 10$ in.; $w = 8$ in.
12. $l = 8$ in.; $w = 6$ in.
13. $l = 37.5$ cm; $w = 30$ cm
14. 2 gal; $35.70
15. 6 gal; $98.10
16. $1,656
17. $9,936
18. $l = 16$ in.; $w = 13.3$ in.
19. $l = 112.5$ cm; $w = 60$ cm

20. 24 square yd; $492

21. 20 square yd; $360

Pages 119-120
Decision Making
1. Intown Bank

2. People's Bank

3. Intown Bank

4. $937.20

5. $910.80

6. $0

7. $850

8. Fixed

9. A.R.M.

10. 30-year

11. 20-year

12. 5.25%

13. 5%

Think About It
1. Because the longer term means you pay much more in interest over the life of the loan.

Page 121
Decision Making
Think About It
1. National Bank (2) has the lower monthly payment, but the closing costs are so much higher than at People's Bank, that People's Bank is actually the better deal.

Page 122
Decision Making
1. The adjustable-rate mortgage has lower closing costs.

2. The adjustable-rate mortgage has the lower rate.

3. The adjustable-rate mortgage is cheaper because it is riskier. The rate might go up after 3 years.

4. Tim and Connie might choose the ARM because they know they will sell the house in 3 years.

5. Answers may vary.

Pages 123-124
Money Tips
1. 5-year ARM

2. 15-year fixed-rate mortgage

3. 30-year fixed-rate mortgage

Think About It
1. $123 per month

2. $34,836.41

Pages 125-126
Estimation Skills
1. 20

2. 300

3. 100

4. 30

5. 10

6. 40

7. 200

8. 200

9. 800

10. 50

11. 5

12. 30

13. 20

14. 9

15. 50

16. 20

17. 6

18. 200

19. 5

20. 30

21. 30

22. 6

23. 60

24. 4

25. 2

26. 9

27. 6

Pages 127-128
Part III Review
1. c

2. b

3. a

4. $420

5. $1,100

6. $133,000

7. $228,850

8. $85,000

9. $460,000

10. $1,004.64

11. $67,500; $471.83

12. $6,520

13. $194,400

14. $89.37

15. $124.10

16. 2 gal.

17. $421

18. $11,882.50

Pages 129-130
Part III Test
1. $425.60

2. $2,088.33

3. $248,180

4. $278,880

5. $22,950; $175,950

6. 1st year: $72,450; $410,550. 2nd year: $61,582.50; $348,967.50

7. $716

8. $15,147; $1057

9. $1,767.05

10. $2,383.50

11. $1,249.60

12. $4,043

13. $184,000; $6,053.60

14. $149,175; $6,101.26

15. $68,500

16. $16,700

17. $155.42

18. $55.60

19. 2

20. $2,992

Support Materials
The Mathematics of Housing and Taxes, SV 9780547625645

CPSIA information can be obtained
at www.ICGtesting.com
Printed in the USA
LVHW060741030922
727547LV00031B/1028